# Contents

## Welcome

**1** **Read and tick (✓).**

**1** Who uses the THD?

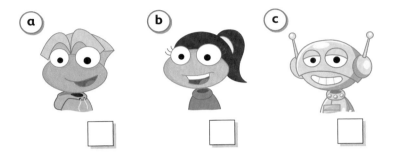

a

b

c

☐ ☐ ☐

**2** Who says she wants to go home?

a

b

c

☐ ☐ ☐

**2** **Read and circle *T* (True) or *F* (False).**

**1** Matt knows the man and the woman who are in his office.     T / F

**2** Matt is tired because it's late at night.     T / F

**3** The mysterious woman doesn't want to leave.     T / F

**4** The THD is working very well.     T / F

**5** Matt and AL time-travel to 1950.     T / F

**6** Bella understands the problem with the THD.     T / F

**3** Who are they? Write.

> AL    Bella    The mysterious couple    Matt

**1**   **2**   **3**   **4**

_____    _____    _____    _____

**4** Look at Activity 3 and number.

**a** He is Matt's robot assistant. He was made with expensive technology. He helps Matt solve difficult problems.  ☐

**b** They came to the Time Park to find a time-travel machine. They took the THD. Now they want to go home. They are clever and fast.  ☐

**c** He is a time engineer. He works in a very modern office. He is hard-working and helpful. He often works very late at night.  ☐

**d** She joins Matt and AL on their mission. She will try to help them find the mysterious couple. She is clever, creative and friendly.  ☐

**5** What do you think is going to happen in the story? Circle.

**1** Matt, AL and Bella will ( help / catch ) the mysterious couple.

**2** Bella ( is going to / is not going to ) stay with Matt and AL until the end of the story.

**3** They can ( time-travel / go by flying car ) to many amazing places.

**4** The mysterious couple ( can / can't ) return to their home happily.

**6** Complete the sentences.

cold   furry   hard   loud   spiky   sweet

**1** The ice is _____.

**2** The chocolate is _____.

**3** The music is _____.

**4** The hair is _____.

**5** The spider is _____.

**6** The rock is _____.

**7** Think and write.

**1** _____Shells are_____ smooth.

**2** _____ round.

**3** _____ soft.

**4** _____ scary.

**5** _____ cute.

**6** _____ loud.

**8** 🎧 1:07 Listen and tick (✓). Then write.

chocolate   a fish   a rose   a stuffed lion

| | looks | feels | smells | sounds | tastes | What is it? |
|---|---|---|---|---|---|---|
| **1** | wet ☐ <br> scary ☐ | rough ☐ <br> cold ☐ | like the sea ☐ <br> like a lemon ☐ | | | _____ |
| **2** | | soft ☐ <br> hard ☐ | | scary ☐ <br> nice ☐ | | _____ |
| **3** | brown ☐ <br> black ☐ | smooth ☐ <br> sharp ☐ | great ☐ <br> bad ☐ | | sour ☐ <br> sweet ☐ | _____ |
| **4** | beautiful ☐ <br> bad ☐ | furry ☐ <br> spiky ☐ | sweet ☐ <br> good ☐ | | | _____ |

**9** **Read and match.**

**1**   AL is made of expensive technology,    **a**   aren't they?

**2**   Bella's hair isn't short,    **b**   isn't he?

**3**   Matt isn't an assistant,    **c**   is it?

**4**   Matt and AL are from the future,    **d**   is he?

**10** **Write about your partner. Then ask and check.**

|   |   | My prediction | ✓ or ✗ |
|---|---|---|---|
| **1** | City/Town | You are from … , aren't you? | |
| **2** | Age | | |
| **3** | Good at | | |
| **4** | Pets | | |
| **5** | Favourite food | | |

**11** **Read and sort. Then write.**

Monday   half an hour   later   tonight   tomorrow

| See you … ! | See you in … ! | See you on … ! |
|---|---|---|
| | | |

**12** **Read and write. What do you say...**

**1**   to your family when you go to school?   _____

**2**   to your friends when you go home?   _____

**3**   to your teachers when classes finish?   _____

**4**   to a friend that you're going to see next week?   _____

# 1 Adventure camp

**1** Put the letters in order to make words. Then number the pictures.

**1** ttne _____

**2** ria mupp _____

**3** geps _____

**4** chort _____

**5** srift dia itk _____

**6** isleengp gba _____

**7** rai sestarmt _____

**8** pomcssa _____

**9** sckaurck _____

a

b

c

d

e

f

g

h

i

**2** Look at Lila's list. Listen and tick (✓) or cross (✗).

**Adventure Camp list**

a rucksack ☐     a compass ☐     books ☐

a torch ☐     an air mattress ☐     a sleeping bag ☐

pegs ☐     an air pump ☐     a first aid kit ☐

**3** Write the words in the correct box.

hiking   torch   tent   sports   compass   kayaking

*What you will do*

*What to bring*

**4 Read and circle.**

1   I like ( play / (playing) ) football, but I ( don't / doesn't ) like camping.

2   He doesn't like ( watch / watching ) TV. He ( like / likes ) reading.

3   We start ( kayak / kayaking ) at ten o'clock. I finish ( having lunch / have lunch ) at about two o'clock.

4   We ( start / starting ) cooking dinner at five o'clock. We finish ( eating / eat ) at seven o'clock.

5   We enjoy ( singing / sing ) and we're good at ( act / acting ).

**5 Make sentences.**

1   Sam / start / playing tennis / nine o'clock. ✗

   _____ .

2   Rachel / finish / singing / eleven o'clock. ✓

   _____ .

3   Andrea / start / dancing / breakfast time. ✗

   _____ .

4   Peter / finish / throwing a ball / dinner time. ✓

   _____ .

**6 Write about yourself.**

My name's _____ .

I'm from _____

in _____ .

I love _____ ,

but I don't like _____ .

I enjoy _____ and _____ ,

but I don't enjoy _____ .

**7** Look and write.

**1**

**2**

**3**

pitch a tent

**4**

**5**

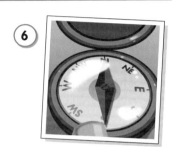

**6**

**8** Look and complete the sentences.

**1** The two boys _are pitching a tent_ . **2** The girl _____.

**3** The man _____. **4** The two girls _____.

**9** Look at the picture in Activity 8. Circle the things that you can see.

cars   compass   campsite   tent   pegs   dog   fire   sky   river

**10**  **Listen and circle.**

**1**   I ( can / can't ) read a book, but I ( can / can't ) read a map.

**2**   They ( can / can't ) swim, but they ( can / can't ) pitch a tent.

**3**   They ( can / can't ) put in the pegs, ( so / and ) they can help pitch the tent.

**4**   She likes reading comic books, ( and / but ) she ( can / can't ) read a compass.

**5**   We ( can / can't ) light a fire, ( so / but ) we can cook dinner, too.

**11**  **Listen and write.**

**Can**

**1**   She can _____ .

**2**   _____

     _____

**3**   _____

     _____

**4**   _____

     _____

**Can't**

**1**   She can't _____ .

**2**   _____

     _____

**3**   _____

     _____

**4**   _____

     _____

**12** **Write.**

What can you do?

_____

_____

_____

What can't you do?

_____

_____

_____

**13** Read and tick (✓).

**1** Who knows where the mysterious couple are going?

a | b | c

**2** Who says they must put out the campfires?

a | b | c

**14** Look at the story. Correct the sentences.

**1** Bella doesn't like camping.

_____

**2** Matt says Bella can't come with them.

_____

**3** They're going to Asia.

_____

**15** Complete. Then number the story events in order.

> Africa    Bella    camp    girl    THD    time-travel

☐ They meet a _____ named Bella.

☐ Matt says that _____ can come with them.

☐ They follow the mysterious couple to _____.

☐ Matt and AL time-travel to an adventure _____.

☐ Bella wants to _____ with Matt and AL.

☐ Bella makes the _____ work again.

**16** **Read and circle.**

**VALUES**

Safety first! Think about safety when you go camping.

**1** You must ( put out a fire / light a fire ) when you leave the campsite.

**2** The campfire ( should / shouldn't be ) close to trees and tents.

**3** You should bring ( fizzy drinks / water ) with you.

**4** You must have ( magazines and music / a first aid kit and sun cream ) with you.

**5** Your rucksack should be ( easy / difficult ) to carry.

**17** **Write two more things you should do to keep safe when you go camping.**

_____

_____

**18**  **Listen and circle the verbs with short vowels.**

**PHONICS & SPELLING**

| | | | |
|---|---|---|---|
| **1** | chatted | stayed | planned | played |
| **2** | shopping | reading | hoping | hopping |
| **3** | stopped | booked | dropped | cooked |
| **4** | surfing | dropping | cutting | getting |

**19** **Read and complete the table.**

| | | | |
|---|---|---|---|
| **1** turn → turned, turning | **2** vote → | **3** shop → |
| **4** work → | **5** stop → | **6** cry → |
| **7** study → | **8** help → | **9** visit → |

## NATURAL SCIENCE

**20** **Read and complete the paragraph.**

humid   dense   droughts   conserving   deforestation

Rainforest are ¹_____ jungles where it rains a lot.
Rainforests are perfect for many plant and animal species to live in because
they are ²_____ . But ³_____ can cause
⁴_____ – a lack of water – which can cause the extinction of
these species. We must start ⁵_____ rainforests to save plants
and animals, and also stop tribes from losing their homes.

**21** **Read and match.**

| | | | |
|---|---|---|---|
| **1** | deforestation | **a** | lack of water |
| **2** | drought | **b** | clearing of forests |
| **3** | habitats | **c** | different weather conditions |
| **4** | climate change | **d** | rivers, seas, rainforests, etc. |

**22** **Read and tick (✓).**

| | | Before deforestation | After deforestation |
|---|---|---|---|
| **1** | drought | | |
| **2** | ten million species of plants and animals | | |
| **3** | hot and humid | | |
| **4** | dense jungle | | |
| **5** | the extinction of plant and animal species | | |
| **6** | climate change | | |

**23** **Find a solution to deforestation. Write.**

**1**   What is necessary to solve the problem? _____

**2**   What can *you* do to solve the problem? _____

# Wider World

**24** **Put the letters in the correct order to make words.**

**1** tnaiounms _____

**2** ldiw _____

**3** thaps _____

**4** cancivol _____

**5** bcain _____

**6** dmu _____

**25** **Complete the sentences. Use the words from Activity 24.**

We like to go camping on a
¹_____ island in Italy. Many people
put ²_____ on their body because
it's good for the skin. We sleep in a small
³_____ and go hiking in the
⁴_____. It's difficult, but it's a lot of
fun. We walk along the ⁵_____ in
small groups. On the way we see many
⁶_____ animals. Camping is fun, so I
go every year.

**26** **Write about your ideal campsite.**

**1** Where is it?

_____

**2** What can you do there?

_____

**3** Why is it ideal for you?

_____

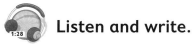 

**27**  **Listen and write.**

Dear Diary,

Adventure Camp is great! It's my third day here. I've got some new friends from ¹_____ and Mexico. They're really nice. I'm teaching ²_____ to my new friend, Eva. She's funny. I like her, but she's not good at learning Spanish! Our first day was good. There was a big dinner, and then there were songs by the campfire. I don't like ³_____, but it was fun. Bed was late, so tonight I want to go to bed early! Yesterday, we ⁴_____ for a walk in the forest. It's very beautiful here. There ⁵_____ any computers, and there ⁶_____ any internet, but I ⁷_____ the camp.

⁸_____ for now,

Pablo

**28** **Look at Activity 27 and answer the questions.**

**WRITING TIP!**

For diaries, we use the pronouns *I, we, my, our.*

We use the past tense to describe what happened, e.g. *We went to bed.*

We use adjectives to describe feelings, e.g. *I felt nervous.*

**1** How does Pablo feel about Adventure Camp?

_____

**2** What did Pablo do on his first day?

_____

**3** What did Pablo do yesterday?

_____

**29** **Read and match.**

| | | | | |
|---|---|---|---|---|
| **1** | first aid kit | **a** | you do this to sleep on the floor |
| **2** | sleeping bag | **b** | you use this to see in the dark |
| **3** | pegs | **c** | this keeps you warm at night |
| **4** | torch | **d** | you can carry clothes and books in this |
| **5** | set up the bed | **e** | you use these to stop a tent from flying away |
| **6** | rucksack | **f** | you need this in case someone is hurt |

**30**  **Listen, circle and number.**

1:30

1 Ron    2 Jo    3 Pablo    4 Jackie

**a**   I can pitch a tent, ( but / and ) I ( can / can't ) read a compass.   ☐

**b**   I like lighting fires, ( but / and ) I ( like / don't like ) cooking.   ☐

**c**   I love hiking with a torch at night, ( but / and ) I ( love / don't love )
camping under the stars.   ☐

**d**   I ( like / don't like ) walking in the rain, ( but / and ) I usually cover my head.   ☐

**31** **Put the words in order to make sentences. Then write *Yes* or *No* for you.**

**1**   like / hiking / I / it's / but / tiring / very

_____ Is it true? _____

**2**   start eating / I / my breakfast / at 6 a.m.

_____ Is it true? _____

**3**   loves / my / fishing / dad

_____ Is it true? _____

I can talk about camping trips and activities using *start*, *finish*,
*enjoy* and *(don't) like* with verb + *–ing*.   ☐ ☐ ☐

I can talk about ability using *can*, *can't*, *so* and *but*.   ☐ ☐ ☐

I can write a diary entry.   ☐ ☐ ☐

# 2 Wildlife park

**1** Put the letters in order to make words. Then match.

a

b

c

d

e

| | |
|---|---|
| **1** trote | _otter_ |
| **2** egrit | _____ |
| **3** sale | _____ |
| **4** tutelr | _____ |
| **5** eawlh | _____ |
| **6** hcthaee | _____ |
| **7** melur | _____ |
| **8** oaalk | _____ |
| **9** orinh | _____ |
| **10** melca | _____ |

f

g

h

i

j

**2** Sort the animals from Activity 1 according to their habitats.

| Jungle/Grassland | River | Sea | Desert |
|---|---|---|---|
| | | | |

**3** Write about the animals in Activity 1.

~~fast~~   scary   heavy   small   slow   big

**1** <u>Cheetahs are fast.</u>          **2** _____

**3** _____          **4** _____

**5** _____          **6** _____

**4**   **Listen and write.**

| | | How tall? | How heavy? | How long? |
|---|---|---|---|---|
| **1** | | 1.2 metres | _250_ kilograms | 2.5 metres |
| **2** | | _____ metres | 60 kilograms | _____ metres |
| **3** | | | _____ kilograms | _____ metres |
| **4** | | _____ metres | _____ kilograms | _____ metres |
| **5** | | _____ metres | _____ kilograms | _____ metres |

**5** **Put the words in order to make questions. Then write answers.**

**1** hippo / is / long / how / the

_____?

_____

**2** the / heavy / elephant / how / is

_____?

_____

**3** long / how / is / the / snake

_____?

_____

**4** cheetah / how / tall / is / the

_____?

_____

**6** **Look at Activity 4 and write sentences about the animals.**

**1** <u>The lion is heavier than the cheetah.</u>

**2** _____

**3** _____

**4** _____

**7** Complete the table.

| | | | | | | |
|---|---|---|---|---|---|---|
| **1** | big | _____ | biggest | **2** | tall | _____ _____ |
| **3** | heavy | _____ _____ | | **4** | slow | _____ _____ |
| **5** | short | _____ _____ | | **6** | small | _____ _____ |
| **7** | fast | _____ _____ | | **8** | light | _____ _____ |
| **9** | long | _____ _____ | | | | |

**8** Look and complete the sentences.

**1** The lemur is faster than the tiger. _____ (fast)

**2** The tiger _____. (big)

**3** The whale _____. (long)

**4** The seal _____. (small)

**5** The otter _____. (heavy)

**6** The turtle _____. (slow)

**9** Complete your own sentences. Then circle the answer that you think is true.

longer faster heavier shorter

**1** Lemurs are _____ than tigers.  Yes, they are. / No, they aren't.

**2** Whales are _____ than seals.  Yes, they are. / No, they aren't.

**3** Whales are _____ than turtles.  Yes, they are. / No, they aren't.

**4** Camels are _____ than otters.  Yes, they are. / No, they aren't.

**10** **Look and answer.**

**1**   Which is the fastest? _____.

**2**   Which is the slowest? _____.

**3**   Which is the best swimmer? _____.

**4**   Which is the heaviest? _____.

**5**   Which is the tallest? _____.

**11** **Make sentences.**

**1**   giraffes / koalas / rhinos (tall)

Giraffes are the tallest. Rhinos are taller than koalas.

**2**   cheetahs / tigers / seals (fast)

_____

**3**   elephants / whales / otters (short)

_____

**4**   butterflies / gorillas / camels (light)

_____

**12** **Write questions about animals. Then swap with a partner and answer their questions.**

rhino   cheetah   koala   lemur   camel   whale   seal   otter   turtle   tiger

**1**   Are rhinos faster than camels? No, a rhino is slower than a camel.

**2**   _____

**3**   _____

**4**   _____

**5**   _____

**13** **Read and tick (✓).**

**1** Who knows a lot about the animals they meet?

**2** Who helps Matt get down from the tree?

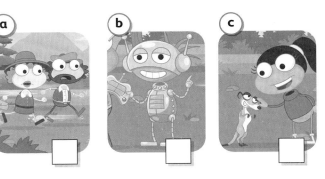

**14** **Correct the sentences.**

**1** The rhino is the fastest animal they see.

_____

**2** Bella calls the cheetah 'little guy.'

_____

**3** They talk to the mysterious couple.

_____

**15** **Complete. Then number the story events in order.**

> arrive   climb   leave   running   says   sees   ties

☐ Matt _____ a cheetah.

☐ They all _____ Africa quickly.

☐ Bella _____ 'hello' to a meerkat.

☐ Matt and Bella _____ a tree.

☐ Bella _____ a knot in her rope, and they get down from the tree.

☐ Matt, Bella and AL _____ in Africa.

☐ The mysterious couple are _____ away from a rhino.

**16** Write about a decision you made and how you made it.

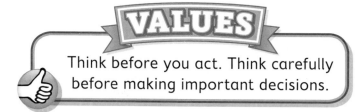

**VALUES**

Think before you act. Think carefully before making important decisions.

**1** I decided to _____

_____ .

**2** Was it a good decision? Why? _____

_____

**17** Match the words in the box with the spelling rules. Then write.

**PHONICS & SPELLING**

| nice   big   new   heavy   happy   late   small   thin |

**1** –er and –est                    _____ and _____

**2** –e + r and –e + st              _____ and _____

**3** –ier / –iest                    _____ and _____

**4** one vowel + one consonant       _____ and _____

**18** Write sentences using the superlative or comparative of the adjectives in Activity 17.

**1**  <u>A rhino is big, but an elephant is the biggest land animal.</u>

**2**  _____

**3**  _____

**4**  _____

**5**  _____

**6**  _____

**7**  _____

**8**  _____

**19** Complete the sentences.

> structure   palaeontologists   dinosaurs   extinct   marine   fossils

**1** _____ lived a long time ago but they are all _____ now.

**2** _____ can find out about the life history of the dinosaurs by studying fossils.

**3** _____ fossils are found under the sea.

**4** _____ are found on every continent on Earth.

**5** They can tell if the animal had fur or not, if it could fly or not and many other details by studying the shape and the _____ of the fossil.

**20** Read and match.

**1** A lot of information can be seen by palaeontologists...

**2** Underwater fossils...

**3** The world's oldest fossil...

**a** ... was found in Quebec, Canada.

**b** ... are found by marine palaeontologists.

**c** ... when a fossil is found.

**21** Look and complete the table.

> fish   pair of wings   butterfly   dinosaur   leaf   insect

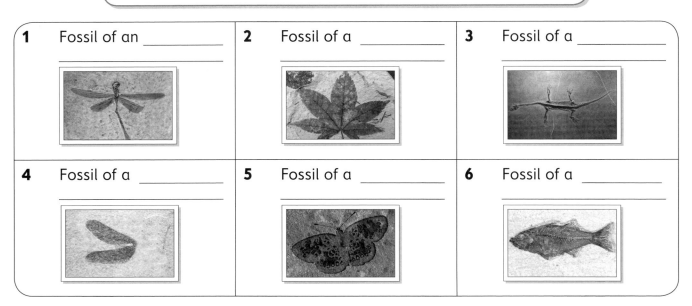

| **1** Fossil of an _____ | **2** Fossil of a _____ | **3** Fossil of a _____ |
| **4** Fossil of a _____ | **5** Fossil of a _____ | **6** Fossil of a _____ |

# Wider World

**22** **Read and match.**

**1** bark

**2** trumpet

**3** hum

**4** snort

**5** roar

**a** noise a lion makes

**b** a low noise like singing with no words

**c** noise a dog makes

**d** nosie an elephant makes that sounds like an instrument

**e** a loud noise through the nose

**23** **Read and complete.**

sound and body   describe   chemicals
flap   communicate   release

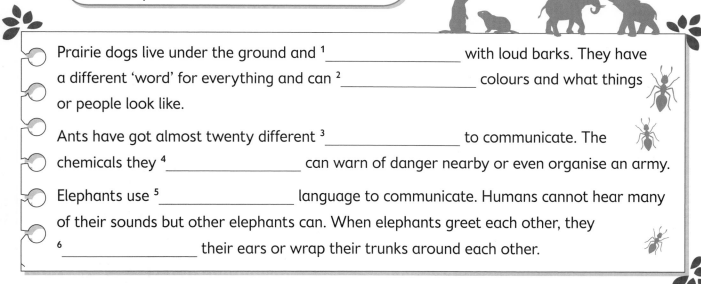

Prairie dogs live under the ground and ¹_____ with loud barks. They have a different 'word' for everything and can ²_____ colours and what things or people look like.

Ants have got almost twenty different ³_____ to communicate. The chemicals they ⁴_____ can warn of danger nearby or even organise an army.

Elephants use ⁵_____ language to communicate. Humans cannot hear many of their sounds but other elephants can. When elephants greet each other, they ⁶_____ their ears or wrap their trunks around each other.

**24** **Think of two other animals you know about. How do they communicate?**

1 _____

2 _____

**25** Write the correct words.

size   body   colour
habitat   food

**WRITING TIP!**

After headings, use a colon (:) to introduce your text, e.g. *Size:*

**WRITING**

**1**   what something looks like   _____

**2**   where something lives   _____

**3**   how big or small something is   _____

**4**   black, yellow, white   _____

**5**   what something eats   _____

**26** Read the sentences. Tick (✓) the ones that can be used in a fact file.

*Wonderful Whales!*

☐   Food: Whales eat fish, krill and tiny shellfish.
They can eat as much as two tonnes of fish a day.

☐   Food: Because whales live in the sea, they eat other fish.
They eat big and small fish and can eat two tonnes a day. My cat likes fish, too!

☐   Body: A male whale has got a very tall fin that looks like a triangle but a female has got a shorter one. It also curves back.

☐   Body: You can tell the difference between a male and a female by looking at their fins. One looks like a triangle and is tall, the other one is shorter and curved.

☐   Group name: Pod (or sometimes school). Whales travel in groups of two or more, and large pods can have more than one hundred whales.

☐   Group name: You can call a group of whales a pod or a school. I think calling them a school of whales is funny.

**27** Use the facts to write sentences for a fact file on whales.

**1**   **Introduction:** over 70 species / one of / smart and noisy animal on Earth

_____

**2**   **Size:** largest / 30 metres long / 173 tonnes / bigger / dinosaurs

_____

**3**   **Habitat:** are in every sea all over world / migrate from cold to warm waters

_____

**28** **Read and circle.**

**1** How ( heavy / heavier ) is the elephant? It's 2,000 ( kilograms / metres ).

**2** How ( long / longer ) is it? It's 2.5 metres ( long / longer ).

**3** The sea turtle is ( bigger / biggest ) than the koala.

**4** Are giraffes ( taller / tallest ) than otters? ( Yes, they are. / No, they aren't. )

**5** Are rhinos ( heavy / heavier ) than lemurs? ( Yes, they are. / No, they aren't. )

**29** **Read and number.**

**a** Which is the heaviest land animal in the world? ☐

**b** Which is the tallest animal in the world? ☐

**c** Which is the fastest land animal in the world? ☐

**d** Which is the longest animal in the world? ☐

**30** **Tick (✓) the correct sentences.**

**1** Fossils are find in many continents. ☐

**2** Flowers are grown in gardens. ☐

**3** The lemur is kept in a wildlife reserve. ☐

**4** Millions of emails are send every day. ☐

**5** Animals are protect in reserves. ☐

**31** **Read and answer.**

**1** What is your favourite animal? _____

**2** What is interesting about it? _____

**3** What is its habitat? _____

**4** What does it eat? _____

**I CAN**

I can ask and answer about animals and make comparisons. ☐ ☐ ☐

I can describe animals using comparative and superlative adjectives. ☐ ☐ ☐

I can write a fact file about an interesting animal. ☐ ☐ ☐

# 3 Where we live

## 1 Find, circle and write.

| f | u | i | t | h | e | a | t | r | e | o | a | x | t |
|---|---|---|---|---|---|---|---|---|---|---|---|---|---|
| a | t | n | o | b | c | b | t | h | e | g | c | p | c |
| c | d | g | c | i | n | e | m | a | p | l | h | r | o |
| t | h | m | d | t | f | s | a | r | j | w | e | z | l |
| o | n | e | w | s | a | g | e | n | t | f | m | h | l |
| r | t | s | t | y | e | k | s | c | s | n | i | n | e |
| y | e | d | e | h | r | v | m | c | q | h | s | u | g |
| s | h | o | p | p | i | n | g | c | e | n | t | r | e |

## 2 Read and match.

**1** newsagent    **a**   This is where you see a film.

**2** cinema    **b**   This is where you can buy newspapers.

**3** post office    **c**   This is where products or goods are made.

**4** college    **d**   This is where you can post a letter.

**5** factory    **e**   This is where you can study after secondary school.

## 3 Complete the sentences.

**1** I can buy medicine in a _____.    **2** I can see clowns and acrobats in a _____.

**3** I buy a magazine in a _____.    **4** I can study in a _____.

**5** I can watch a film in a _____.    **6** I can buy some clothes in a _____.

**4**  **Listen and write.**

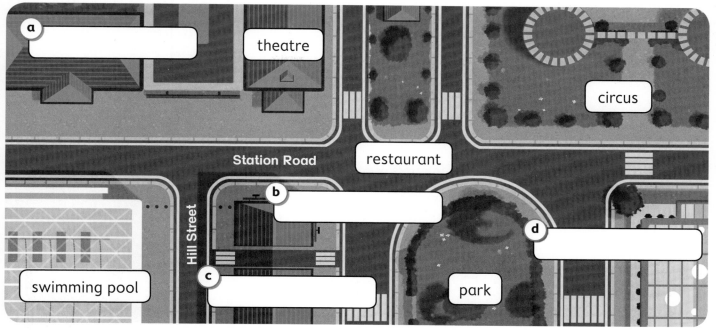

a

theatre

circus

Station Road

restaurant

b

d

Hill Street

swimming pool

c

park

**5** **Look at the map in Activity 4 and write.**

**1** cinema / swimming pool    <u>The cinema is opposite the swimming pool.</u>

**2** theatre / cinema    _____

**3** chemist / restaurant    _____

**4** park / shopping centre    _____

**5** circus / park    _____

**6** **Draw a map showing how you get from home to school. Then write.**

**7** Put the letters in order to make words. Then match.

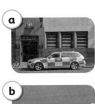

1   eirf attsion    _____

2   praroit    _____

3   tuesg ushoe    _____

4   ndrgrndueou    _____

5   oieplc aiosttn    _____

6   pooshokb    _____

**8** Read and match.

1   This is where you call when there's a fire.

2   This is where you call when there's an emergency.

3   This is where you can stay when you visit a new place.

4   This is where you can see your favourite sport.

5   This is where you wait for your bus.

a   bus stop

b   fire station

c   stadium

d   guest house

e   police station

**9**  1:55   Listen and complete.

bookshop   bus stop   fire station
police station   university

**Katy:**   Hello?

**Michael:**   Hi, Katy! How are you? It's Michael here.

**Katy:**   Oh! Hi, Michael! I'm fine, thank you. How are you?

**Michael:**   Oh, fine, thanks. I'm just looking for the [1]_____ that you told me about. I'm in front of the [2]_____ and I can't find it. Can you help me?

**Katy:**   Of course! Can you see the [3]_____?

**Michael:**   Let me see...

**Katy:**   There's a [4]_____ and a police station. Can you see them?

**Michael:**   Yes. Now I can see them.

**Katy:**   Just walk straight ahead and you will find it on the right. It's very close to the [5]_____.

**Michael:**   Oh, I can see it now. Thank you very much.

**Katy:**   You're welcome. See you tomorrow.

**Michael:**   Bye!

**10** **Read and find the mistakes. Then write correct sentences.**

**1** If I can go to the supermarket, I can buy some food.

**2** So you need help, you can go to the police station.

**3** If Mary wants to be early, she should to take a taxi.

**4** If you to want a new book, you should go to the bookshop.

**11** **Complete the sentences with the correct form of the verbs. Use *should* and *can*.**

**1** If I _____ (travel) to London, I _____ (take) a map with me.

**2** If you _____ (need) a place to stay, you _____ (try) the guest house.

**3** You _____ (get lost) in a city, if you _____ (turn) the wrong way.

**4** If you _____ (go) to the post office, you _____ (buy) some stamps.

**5** You _____ (travel) faster if you _____ (use) the underground.

**6** If you _____ (live) in a city, you _____ (do) lots of things.

**12** **Complete the sentences with your own ideas.**

**1** If I go to the shopping centre, I can _____.

**2** If we go to Paris, we should _____.

**3** _____, I can wake up early in the morning.

**4** If it's sunny, we should _____.

**5** _____, I can use my umbrella.

**6** If we want to exercise, _____.

**13** **Read and tick (✓).**

**1**   Who wants to go to the control centre?

**2**   Who sees that someone is coming?

**14** **Read and circle.**

**1**   AL ( knows / doesn't know ) what Dot and Zeb Martin are looking for.

**2**   Dot and Zeb Martin are trying to ( buy / take ) a space-time chip.

**3**   Matt wants to ( eat something / find something ).

**15** **Complete the summary.**

> Atlantis   chip   control centre   hungry   security guard   time-travel

Zeb and Dot Martin go to ¹_____. Matt, Bella and AL follow them.
They see a video of the Martins in the ²_____. AL says the Martins
are looking for a space-time ³_____. The chip is important for a
⁴_____ machine. A ⁵_____ comes and they hide. Matt
is ⁶_____, and he thinks the Martins are, too.

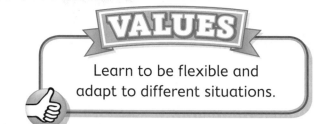

**VALUES**

Learn to be flexible and adapt to different situations.

**16** **Read these situations.**
**Write how you could be flexible.**

**1** You want to go shopping, but your friend hasn't got any money.

<u>I could think of a fun, free activity to do this weekend, and ask</u>
<u>my friend to come shopping with me next weekend.</u>

**2** You want to go to a party, but you have to be home before 10 p.m.

_____

**3** You want to meet your friends, but you have to study for a test.

_____

**4** You want to stay up late, but you have to get up early.

_____

**5** You want to watch an action film, but your friend wants to watch a comedy.

_____

**17** **Read and circle the words with suffixes.**

**PHONICS & SPELLING**

**1** Our guide was very friendly.

**2** She played with the kitten carefully.

**3** 'Can I help you?' she asked kindly.

**4** You should talk politely to older people.

**5** He ran quickly to catch the bus.

**6** I visit my grandparents regularly.

**18** **Look, sort and write.**

care
friend
quick
love
strange

month
play
careful
beauty
easy
peace

| Noun + –ful | Noun + –ly | Adjective + –ly |
|-------------|------------|-----------------|
|             | friendly   |                 |

**19** Complete the sentences.

> population   urban   village   traffic   dirty

**1**   There is a lot of _____ where I live – everyone drives a car!

**2**   People who live in a city are called the _____ population.

**3**   The current world _____ is 7.6 billion people!

**4**   The streets in cities can sometimes be _____ – people throw a lot of rubbish.

**5**   My grandad lives in a _____. It's much smaller than a town and there is only one newsagent.

**20**   Read the information below and complete the chart.

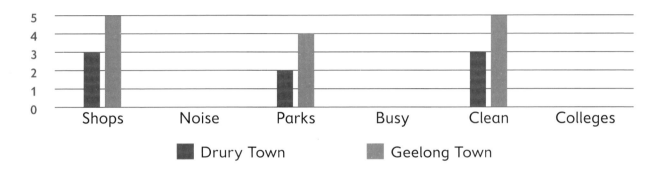

✿ Drury Town hasn't got as many shops as Geelong Town. Drury Town has got three shops but Geelong Town has got five.

✿ Drury Town is as noisy as Geelong Town. They both score 3 out of 5.

✿ Drury Town hasn't got as many parks as Geelong Town. Drury Town has got two parks but Geelong Town has got four parks.

✿ Drury Town is as busy as Geelong Town. They both score 2 out of 5.

✿ Drury Town isn't as clean as Geelong Town. Drury Town scores 3 out of 5 but Geelong Town scores 5 out of 5.

✿ Geelong Town has got as many colleges as Drury Town. They have both got four colleges.

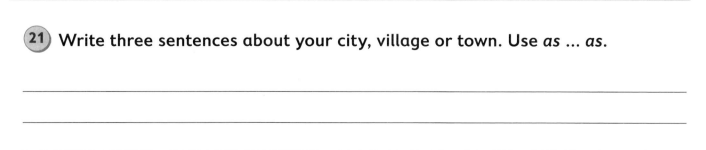

**21**   Write three sentences about your city, village or town. Use *as ... as*.

_____

_____

_____

# Wider World

**22** **Read and sort.**

**Petra - 12** I'm from a Greek island called Santorini. We've got a small local population, but a lot of tourists. My house is unusual because it's a cave house! It is painted blue and white, and is cool in the summer. The capital city, Fira, has got nice shops and cafes. An interesting fact is that Santorini sits on top of a volcano!

**Amir - 12** I live in Sydney, Australia, It's a very big city with lots of parks. I love going to Hyde Park in the centre of the city. I ride my bike there or skateboard. There is a big urban population and many people live in tall buildings. An interesting fact about Sydney is that it has got an underground lake!

**Cathy - 13** I live in a fishing village called Kas in Turkey. It hasn't got many people but there are lots of activities to do. The houses are white with pretty pink flowers that grow around the doors. They are very cute. We have got a beach, and lots of people go diving. An interesting fact is that there is an underwater plane that you can swim inside!

| Place | Homes | Things to see/do | Interesting fact |
|---|---|---|---|
| Santorini, Greece | | | |
| | | | |
| | | | |

**23** **Write a flyer about your city or town.**

- What are some great things to see and do?
- What is interesting about the place where you live?

_____
_____
_____
_____

**24** 🎧 2:05 **Listen and number the sentences in order.**

**a** Do you want to come to Seoul in the summer? ☐

**b** I don't like quiet places! ☐

**c** I live near a big park with a lot of trees and flowers. ☐

**d** I want to be good at everything! ☐

**e** Thanks for your email. It was really interesting! ☐

Alex

Sun-kwan

**25** 🎧 2:06 **Circle. Then listen again and check your answers.**

**1** Alex ( wants / doesn't want ) to know more about Seoul.

**2** Sun-kwan ( likes / doesn't like ) quiet places.

**3** There's a river ( opposite / behind ) Sun-kwan's house.

**4** Sun-kwan ( wants / doesn't want ) to go to Sark one day.

**26** **Complete the sentences with _and, but_ or _because_.**

**1** I don't like the city _____ it's too noisy.

**2** She wants to go to bed _____ she's tired.

**3** He likes going to the library, _____ he doesn't like going to the castle.

**4** My town is clean, _____ it isn't beautiful.

**5** I like surfing _____ snorkelling.

**WRITING TIP!**

We use _and_ to join two similar or related ideas, e.g. _There is a post office and a newsagent._

We use _but_ to join a positive and a negative idea, e.g. _We play sports, but sometimes there aren't enough people._

We use _because_ to give a reason, e.g. _I'm happy because my family and friends are here._

**27** **Write about where you live.**

I like where I live because _____

_____

_____

_____

**28** **Read and circle.**

**I CAN DO IT!**

**1**   If you want to buy books, you should go to the ( bookshop / college ).

**2**   If you want to travel to Europe, you can go to the ( fire station / airport ).

**3**   You should go to the ( supermarket / post office ) if you need to buy food.

**4**   You can go to the ( shopping centre / railway station ) if you need new shoes.

**5**   If you want to watch the football match, you can go to the ( theatre / stadium ).

**29** **Answer the questions for you.**

**1**   What can you see where you live? _____

**2**   What do you like best about where you live? _____

**3**   What places do you usually go to? _____

**30** **Look at the map and answer the questions.**

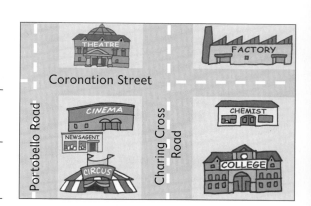

**1**   How do you get to the factory from the college?

_____

**2**   How do you get to the newsagent from the chemist?

_____

**3**   How do you get to the factory from the circus?

_____

**31** **Your friend has got some questions. What do you say?
Answer using *If* and *can* or *should*.**

**1**   I want to see a film.

_____

**2**   I need to buy some stamps.

_____

**3**   I want to study a new subject.

_____

**I CAN**

I can say where places are and give directions.

I can use *if* sentences to give directions and advice.

I can write a friendly email about a place.

# 4 Good food, good mood

**1** Look and complete. Then write Flo's favourite food.

My favourite food is _____.

**2** Answer the questions using *every day/week*, *sometimes* or *never*.

**1** How often do you eat spaghetti? **2** How often do you eat fish?

_____ _____

**3** How often do you eat fruit? **4** How often do you eat biscuits?

_____ _____

**3** Answer for you.

**1** Describe your favourite food.

_____

**2** What dish is your country famous for? Give a short description.

_____

**4** Write the verbs in the past.

**1** climb ___climbed___   **2** cook _____   **3** drop _____

**4** want _____   **5** visit _____   **6** fall _____

**7** sail _____   **8** eat _____

**5** Complete with words from Activity 4.

**1**

I _____ Mount Everest last year.

**2**

We _____ paella yesterday. It was difficult!

**3**

He _____ the plate on his foot. Ouch!

**6** Read and complete.

was   loved   went   wanted   ate

Yesterday was a good day! A lot of people ¹_____ to the lake to do sports and I went with them. There was swimming, snorkelling and kayaking. I ²_____ scared at first, but I ³_____ kayaking. It was exciting! I ⁴_____ to do it all day. I was with Tom and we paddled very quickly around the lake. There was a race with Flo and Maria, and Tom was the winner. After our day at the lake, we had omelettes and salad for dinner. I ⁵_____ my dinner very quickly because I was really hungry!

**7** Look at Activity 6 and answer the questions.

**1** Did Maria win the race? _____

**2** Did they have curry for dinner? _____

## 8 Circle. Then look and match.

**1** prepared ( the ingredients / a recipe )

**2** washed ( a list / the dishes )

**3** turned on ( the food / the oven )

**4** served ( a meal / the dishes )

**5** read ( a recipe / the meal )

**6** had ( a list / a meal )

**7** bought ( food / the dishes )

**8** made ( the oven / a list )

## 9 Read and circle.

**1** Last night I ( make / made ) a nice salad.

**2** We ( had / didn't have ) paella for lunch on Saturday. It was very tasty!

**3** I ( lost / didn't lose ) the shopping list. I couldn't remember all the ingredients.

**4** When I ( turn / turned ) on the oven, I burnt my hand.

**5** The lights ( go / went ) out last night.

**6** I ( washed / didn't wash ) the dishes. Dad said thank you!

## 10 Complete the sentences with the past form of the verbs.

**1** My brother _____ (not wash) the dishes. I was angry because I _____ (prepare) the meal!

**2** Mum _____ (serve) the food, but she _____ (not turn on) the oven. The dinner was cold!

**3** I _____ (make) a list and _____ (buy) the ingredients. We got everything we needed.

**4** Grandad _____ (not read) the recipe properly. He added too much salt. Grandma _____ (not like) the meal.

**11** **2:17** **Listen and number.**

**a**

**b**

**c**

**d**

**12** Look at the pictures in Activity 11. What happened? Write sentences using *when* and *while*.

**a** _____

**b** _____

**c** _____

**d** _____

**13** Write sentences about yourself. What happened?

> walk home    do my homework    make a salad    watching TV

**1** _____ when _____ .

**2** _____ while _____ .

**3** _____ when _____ .

**4** _____ while _____ .

**14** Read and tick (✓).

**1** Who didn't eat any food?

**2** Who didn't like the meerkat?

---

**15** Correct the sentences.

**1** Zeb didn't like the dumplings.

_____

**2** Dot knew what the meerkat was.

_____

**3** Dot and Zeb didn't take the rubbish bin of old food.

_____

---

**16** Complete. Then number the story events in order.

> asked    ate    left    looked    made    thought

☐ Dot _____ in a rubbish bin.

☐ Dot _____ the meerkat was a rat.

☐ Matt, Bella, and the meerkat _____ some food.

☐ Dot and Zeb _____ the restaurant with the rubbish bin.

☐ The chef _____ dumplings for Zeb.

☐ Zeb _____ Dot what happened.

**17** **What should they do? Look at the suggestions. Write sentences.**

call a friend    eat something you like
go swimming    go to the cinema
meet some friends    play some games
rest    talk to someone    watch TV

VALUES
Relaxing is important.

**1**    My mum keeps telling me to stop being lazy.

_____

**2**    I studied all day today. I'm really tired.

_____

**3**    I feel lonely. I've got nothing to do at home.

_____

**4**    I didn't have time to have lunch today.

_____

**18**   2:21  **Listen, sort and write.**

PHONICS & SPELLING

played    visited    cooked    decided    washed    followed    cleaned    landed    dropped
collected    stopped    remembered    recorded    brushed    studied    revised    listened
watched    sounded    pitched    tasted    walked    covered    asked

| / t / sound | / id / sound | / d / sound |
|---|---|---|
| | | |
| | | |
| | | |
| | | |
| | | |

**19** **Read and circle in red for /t/, blue for /d/ and green for /id/.**

**1**    I packed my bag in three minutes!    **2**    She missed the bus and waited for one hour.

**3**    He dropped the plate yesterday.    **4**    His spaghetti tasted delicious.

**5**    We cooked together in the classroom.    **6**    They borrowed the recipe from their aunt.

**20** Read and complete.

> balanced    exercise    lifestyle    physical    portions    energy

Having a healthy ¹_____ is not as difficult as you think.
²_____ is very important. Walking or cycling, instead of sitting in the car, is
one way to make sure you do enough ³_____ activity. It's also important to
have a ⁴_____ diet and eat a lot of fruit and vegetables. We can get nutrients
from meat and fish, but we shouldn't eat large ⁵_____. We should eat fewer
fats, too. If you eat well and get plenty of exercise, you have more ⁶_____.

**21** Read and circle. Then complete the questions.

**1**    Sam ( did / didn't ) have a lot of energy, _____ *did she* _____?

**2**    Sam ( was / wasn't ) doing a lot of physical activity, _____?

**3**    Sam ( was /wasn't ) eating a balanced diet, _____?

**4**    Sam ( did / didn't ) improve her lifestyle, _____?

**22** Complete the questions with words from Activity 20. Then find out
the answers.

**1**    How many _____ of fruit and vegetables should we eat each day?

    _____

**2**    What other foods make a _____ diet?

    _____

**3**    What is the correct amount of _____ we should do each day?

    _____

**4**    How much _____ (kj) does an egg give us?

    _____

**23** Now write three things you could do to improve your health.

_____

_____

_____

# Wider World

**24** **Read and complete.**

> more slowly   apps   minerals   ingredients   healthy diet

There are many ways to be healthy. Firstly, it's important to have a ¹_____.
Diets packed with vegetables, beans and lentils are rich in ²_____ and iron.
It's also important to have a diet that balances smaller amounts of meat and dairy with lots
of fruit and vegetables, like the Mediterranean diet. Eating with chopsticks also helps you eat
³_____, as research has shown that fast eaters eat more. You can monitor how
much you eat with new and fun ⁴_____ like *Foodwatch*. It helps you watch what
you eat and gives you a score for vitamins and minerals. For example, fish is good for your brain.
Other apps like *RecipeMaker* suggest healthy meals with few ⁵_____ .

**25** **Look at Activity 24 and answer the questions.**

**1** What has research shown about fast eaters?

_____

**2** Why is the Mediterranean diet one of the best?

_____

**3** Which food is good for our brain?

_____

**4** What technology can help you see how many vitamins and minerals are in your food?

_____

**26** **Compare the traditional diet in your country with the Mediterranean diet.
What is similar? What is different?**

**1** In my country, the traditional diet is _____.

**2** It is similar to the Mediterranean diet because _____.

**3** It is different to the Mediterranean diet because _____.

**4** Both the Mediterranean diet and my diet _____.

**(27) Read and write S for similarities and D for differences.**

**A** ☐ The main difference between a cookery show and a recipe book is that you watch one and read the other.

**B** ☐ There are many cookery shows on the internet and there are also free recipe books you can download, or websites with different recipes.

**C** ☐ In both cookery shows and recipe books you learn about different ways to cook.

**D** ☐ Both cookery shows and recipes books have information about ingredients and the amounts you need.

**E** ☐ Both can also show you how you can cook the same food in different ways.

**F** ☐ On cookery shows they show you what the ingredients look like, but in recipe books they give you a list.

**(28) Think about the following places and things. How are they similar? How are they different? Write sentences.**

> **WRITING TIP!**
>
> For describing similarities:
> *The photos are similar because...*
> *In both photos...*
>
> For describing differences:
> *The main difference...*
> *One photo... , but the other... .*

**1** newsagent / book shop

<u>A newsagent is similar to a bookshop because they both sell things to read.</u>

**2** cinema / theatre

_____

**3** school / college

_____

**4** paella / rice and beans

_____

**5** fruit / vegetables

_____

**(29) Look at Activity 28. Choose one pair of items and write a paragraph on how they are similar and how they are different.**

_____

_____

_____

**30** **Read and match.**

1   curry                          **a**   a dish made with eggs
2   stew                           **b**   a hot and spicy food from India
3   spaghetti                      **c**   fish and rice – popular in Japan
4   fish and chips                 **d**   rice and seafood – popular in Spain
5   sushi                          **e**   meat and vegetables cooked slowly
6   paella                         **f**   a type of pasta
7   omelette                       **g**   a popular food in England

**31**  **Listen and number. Then write.**

**a**   She _____ the _____ yesterday.

**b**   They _____ a big _____ last year.

**c**   We _____ stew for _____ today.

**32** **Complete the questions.**

1   He's from England, __isn't he?__          **2**   You didn't play football, _____?

3   You're twelve, _____?           **4**   The dinner was good, _____?

**33**  **Complete with the past form of the verbs.**

Last week I had a birthday party. I ¹_____ (make) a list of friends to invite. Dad
²_____ (look) online for a cake recipe. While he ³_____ (prepare)
the ingredients, he ⁴_____ (see) a mouse. He ⁵_____ (drop) the bowl
with the cake mixture! He ⁶_____ (jump) up and down when Mum arrived. Mum
⁷_____ (buy) a wonderful cake from the supermarket. She brought it out while
everyone ⁸_____ (sing) Happy Birthday!

**I CAN**

I can talk about things that happened or didn't happen in the past.

I can describe past events using the past simple and continuous.

I can write a text describing similarities and differences between two things.

# 5 Arts and entertainment

**1** Look and write the types of film.

**1**

_____

**2**

_____

**3**

_____

**4**

_____

**5**

_____

**6**

_____

**2** Read and circle.

**1** This is a ( fantasy / biography ) about the life of Queen Elizabeth.

**2** Detective Tom Jones is back in this ( action / mystery ) film about the missing jewels.

**3** Jason Statton is amazing as Policeman Smith in his new ( romance / action ) film.

**4** Witches, fairies and trolls are all in Jo Pott's new ( fantasy / sci-fi ) film.

**3** Write about yourself. Then compare with your partner.

| I like these types of films. | I dislike these types of films. |
| --- | --- |
|  |  |

Both my partner and I like _____ films.

Neither of us like _____ films.

**4** Read and circle.

**1** We haven't been to the supermarket ( already / yet ).

**2** Jane and Kate ( have never asked / never asked ) the teacher so many questions.

**3** She ( already / never ) tidied her room – she did it yesterday!

**4** Have the children ( ever / yet ) eaten dumplings?

**5** We've ( never / ever ) seen a rhino at the zoo.

**5** Look and make sentences. Use *already* or *yet*.

**1** Tim ✗ make _____

**2** Gemma ✓ see _____

**3** Freddie and Frida ✗ have _____

**4** Flo ✓ write in _____

**6** Complete the sentences with the correct form of the verbs.

**1** The boy _____ (write) an email to a friend.

**2** Tonya _____ (never / eat) Chinese food.

**3** The children _____ (see) the new comedy film.

**4** I _____ (not / make) my school sandwiches yet.

**5** They _____ (already / have) dinner.

**6** The teacher _____ (open) all the windows.

**7** Complete the sentences for you.

**1** I have never _____.

**2** I have already _____.

**3** I _____ yet.

**8** Read and sort. What family do these instruments belong to?

cello   harmonica   saxophone   cymbal   drums   clarinet   harp   tambourine

| Percussion | Wind | String |
|---|---|---|
|  |  |  |

**9** Read and match.

| | | | | |
|---|---|---|---|---|
| **1** | classical | **a** | smooth with saxophones and trumpets |
| **2** | jazz | **b** | traditional, with harmonicas and tambourines |
| **3** | folk | **c** | relaxing, with harps and cellos |
| **4** | opera | **d** | mixing talking and singing |
| **5** | rap | **e** | singing in high or low voices |

**10** Read and complete.

tambourine   sing   drums   jazz   trumpet   concert

**Bryn:** Did you play the clarinet at the school _____?

**Michelle:** No, I didn't. I played the _____.

**Bryn:** Did Jack play the _____? He's good at percussion!

**Michelle:** Yes, he did. We played _____ music together.

**Bryn:** Did Alice _____? She's your singer, isn't she?

**Michelle:** Yes, that's right. She played the _____ with her hands, too!

**11** Write about yourself. Then compare with a partner.

jazz   rock   opera   pop   folk   reggae   rap   classical music

| I like these types of music. | I dislike these types of music. |
|---|---|
|  |  |

We both like _____ music.   Neither of us like _____.

**12** Read and sort.

| three years   a week   then   June   last week   now   two days   I was six |

| since | for | just |
|-------|-----|------|
|       |     |      |

**13** Read and match.

1 Andy has worked on the project

2 Blake has just

3 Maria hasn't seen Jane since

4 Lucy's sister has

5 The shopping centre has

6 Frankie has visited the shopping centre three times

a finished the project.

b been ill since Monday.

c for five days.

d last month.

e just opened.

f since Thursday.

**14** Complete the sentences.

| yet   just   since   already   for |

1 I've wanted that album _____ a long time!

2 Have you seen my MP3 player? I haven't seen it _____ I left it on the table.

3 I've _____ remembered where I saw that film.

4 Have you finished? No, I haven't. Not _____.

5 I've _____ read that book. I read it last year at school.

**15** Complete the sentences for you.

1 I _____ for _____.

2 I _____ since _____.

3 I have just _____.

**16** **Read and tick (✓).**

**1** Who works in the recording studio?

**2** Who made some music?

**17** **Complete. Then number the story events in order.**

cupboard   'help'   music   saxophone   studio   trace

AL found a _____ and AL, Matt and Bella left the studio.

Bella, Matt and AL arrived at the _____, but the Martins weren't there.

The studio manager listened to the _____ that the Martins recorded.

The studio manager told Matt that the Martins took a _____.

They found the studio manager in a _____.

They heard the studio manager call _____.

**18** **What has happened in the story so far? Circle _T_ (True) or _F_ (False).**

**1** Matt and AL met Bella at an adventure camp.          T / F

**2** Matt and Bella talked to the Martins in Africa.          T / F

**3** Dot and Zeb went to Atlantis to find a space-time chip.          T / F

**4** Dot and Zeb took a rubbish bin from the restaurant.          T / F

**5** The studio manager recorded the Martins playing music.          T / F

**6** The studio manager gave the Martins a saxophone.          T / F

**19** **Plan how to revise for an English test. Number in order.**

**a** Ask a friend to revise with you. ☐

**b** Plan the work, and when and where to meet. ☐

**c** Read the LOOK! boxes and check we understand them. ☐

**d** Find examples of the grammar in each unit. ☐

**e** Meet at the school library. ☐

**20** 2:39 **Listen. Then mark rising intonation (↗) or falling intonation (↘).**

**PHONICS & SPELLING**

( ↗ rising intonation ) ( ↘ falling intonation )

**1** She isn't having dinner with us, is she? ☐

**2** John came to the party, didn't he? ☐

**3** It's cold today, isn't it? ☐

**4** You are visiting your grandad, aren't you? ☐

**5** They didn't enjoy the party, did they? ☐

**6** It isn't a very good film, is it? ☐

**21** **Complete the questions.**

**1** You are coming with us, _____ aren't you? _____

**2** This book is very boring, _____ ?

**3** You revised a lot for the test, _____ ?

**4** She doesn't play the piano, _____ ?

**5** It is a very hot day, _____ ?

**6** You like the new teacher, _____ ?

**7** They won't go on holiday this summer, _____ ?

**8** He would like a cup of coffee, _____ ?

**22** **Read and match.**

| | | | | |
|---|---|---|---|---|
| **1** | Pop music | **a** | started in Jamaica. |
| **2** | Rock | **b** | is influenced by African music. |
| **3** | Reggae | **c** | was very popular in the 1970s in the USA. |
| **4** | Blues | **d** | is short for popular music. |
| **5** | Country music | **e** | is played with the guitar, drum and bass. |

**23** **Answer for you.**

| | |
|---|---|
| What is your favourite kind of music? | |
| Have you ever been to a pop concert? | |
| Have you ever met a famous singer? | |
| Have you ever played the trumpet? | |
| Has your favourite group ever sung in your city/town? | |

**24** **Read the text again on Pupil's Book page 62 and circle *T* (True) or *F* (False).**

**1** Blues was born in the United Kingdom. T / F

**2** Country singers usually write their own songs. T / F

**3** There is only one type of rock music. T / F

**4** Pop music is popular with young people. T / F

**5** Blues was influenced by music from Africa. T / F

**6** Folk and gospel are the roots of country music. T / F

**7** Pop music isn't commercial music. T / F

# Wider World

**25** Read the texts about musical instruments. Look at the photos and circle.

The Oud is a popular ( string / percussion ) musical instrument in the Middle East, Africa and Greece. It has got ten, eleven or thirteen ( strings / drums ) and it is made of wood. This musical instrument is played on special occasions and at family parties. In museums, we see pictures of Ancient Egyptians playing this instrument.

The accordion is a German instrument and it is almost two hundred and fifty years old. It isn't very big, but it is heavy and it looks like a small ( piano / harp ). It is made of wood and metal and you play it with both hands. You play the keys with one hand and you press the buttons with the other. As you play, you push and pull the accordion to make music. Some accordions have got thirty-seven or forty-one keys and many ( buttons / strings ). The Germans play it during traditional holidays and on special occasions.

The didgeridoo is a long pipe and it is made of ( wood / goat's skin ). Some pipes are three metres long. The longer a didgeridoo is, the deeper the sound. We don't know how old didgeridoos are exactly, but drawings on rocks show that they could be 1,500 years old. You have to ( sit down / stand up ) to play the didgeridoo. Aboriginal people play this instrument during special ceremonies like weddings and funerals.

**26** Look at Activity 25 and complete the table.

| Name of the instrument | Country | Materials | When do people play it? |
|---|---|---|---|
|  |  |  |  |
|  |  |  |  |
|  |  |  |  |

**27** Read and match.

## Application

| | | | | |
|---|---|---|---|---|
| **1** | Name: | **a** | Drama __ Dance __ Film ✓ |
| **2** | Length of course: | **b** | Marcelo Iglessas |
| **3** | Email: | **c** | mci@hotpost.com |
| **4** | Course: | **d** | I enjoy watching films and making short films for the internet. I like all types of film, but my favourite type is action films. I want to be a director one day. |
| **5** | Why should we choose you? | **e** | two weeks |

**28** Tick (✓) the things you would answer in an application form for film school.

**1** ☐ name                **2** ☐ address

**3** ☐ your pet's name      **4** ☐ your favourite food

**5** ☐ your preference      **6** ☐ write what you can do (if they ask)

**7** ☐ write about your favourite sport (if they ask)      **8** ☐ write why they should choose you (if they ask)

**29** Complete the application form for a film school.

Name: _____

Age: _____

What types of films do you like? _____
_____

Why should we choose you? _____
_____
_____
_____

**WRITING TIP**

Remember to fill in all relevant sections of the application form. If you don't have information to put in a section you can write: *N/A* (not applicable).

# I CAN DO IT!

## 30 Read and match.

1  You blow this instrument, and it is very small.
2  A percussion instrument that you have to hit.
3  You can shake this or hit it.
4  This is a large string instrument.
5  This is a metal instrument that has got three sides.
6  You blow into this instrument to make sound.

a  cello
b  harmonica
c  triangle
d  clarinet
e  drums
f  tambourine

## 31 Put the words in order to make sentences or questions.

1  concert / ever / played / you / a / in / music / have / ?

_____

2  never / concert / I / a / been / pop / have / to / .

_____

3  someone / you / ever / famous / met / have / ?

_____

4  swum / ocean / an / haven't / in / I / yet / .

_____

## 32 Read and find the mistakes. Then write correct sentences.

1  I have worked here since two months.

_____

2  We haven't finished our test just.

_____

3  They have ever seen a whale.

_____

## 33 Write a few sentences about your favourite types of film or music.

_____

_____

### I CAN

I can talk about different types of film and musical instruments.

I can talk about what I have and haven't done.

I can complete an application form with personal details.

# 6 Trips

## 1 Look and write.

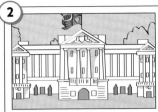

_____  _____  _____  _____

_____  _____  _____  _____

## 2 Complete the sentences. Use the words from Activity 1.

**1**  We went to the _____. There were a lot of fish there.

**2**  The _____ was great. We camped on Friday and Saturday night.

**3**  We loved the _____ because we love swimming.

**4**  The _____ was great! We climbed over the old walls.

**5**  The _____ was fun. I was sometimes scared, but it was exciting!

**6**  The _____ was interesting, but the queen wasn't there.

**7**  I liked the _____. There were lots of dinosaurs there!

**8**  I got dizzy when I looked down from the top floor of the _____.

## 3 Write about yourself. Use words from Activity 1.

I love going to the _____ and _____.

I like _____,

but I don't like _____.

**4** **Read and match.**

**1** What will you do at the library?

**2** What will you do at the botanical gardens?

**3** What will you do at the sports stadium?

**4** What will you do at the museum?

**5** What will you do at the aquarium?

**6** What will you do at the national park?

**a** I'll take pictures of the flowers.

**b** First, I'll get some books for school. Then, I'll go on the internet.

**c** First, I'll go to the dinosaur room. Then, I'll go to the insect room.

**d** I'll see lots of beautiful fish.

**e** First, I'll pitch the tent. Then, I'll go hiking.

**f** I'll watch a football match.

**5** **Look and write.**

~~snorkelling~~ rollerblading horse riding
skateboarding rock climbing surfing

**1**

First, I'll go _____ snorkelling _____ .

Then, I'll go _____ .

**2**

First, _____ .

Then, _____ .

**3**

_____

_____

**6** **Put the words in the correct order to make questions. Then answer.**

**1** what / will / after / do / you / school _____ ?

_____

**2** go / weekend / where / will / you / at / the _____ ?

_____

**3** your / on / trip / will / go / where / you _____ ?

_____

**7** **Write about a partner. Use the questions in Activity 6.**

_____

**8** Look and write. Then find.

1 _____

2 _____

3 _____

4 _____

5 _____

6 _____

| a | r | o | l | l | e | r | c | o | a | s | t | e | r |
|---|---|---|---|---|---|---|---|---|---|---|---|---|---|
| p | t | i | n | i | a | m | i | n | i | g | o | l | f |
| i | z | b | b | e | r | c | f | p | q | j | d | i | g |
| r | b | l | o | r | b | i | g | w | h | e | e | l | k |
| a | f | s | a | r | e | m | v | a | w | y | z | t | k |
| t | f | n | t | g | o | s | d | t | c | l | u | s | c |
| e | d | k | i | q | a | h | i | e | e | d | h | n | l |
| s | o | i | n | g | b | c | a | r | o | u | s | e | l |
| h | d | l | g | f | n | x | d | s | o | b | e | v | t |
| i | g | m | l | n | f | w | m | l | f | b | n | k | j |
| p | e | w | a | t | b | k | u | i | r | g | u | p | x |
| x | m | o | k | y | j | c | u | d | l | v | m | w | t |
| p | s | z | e | a | b | b | l | e | b | w | a | t | s |

**9** There are two more rides in Activity 8.
Find them and complete the sentences.

My favourite ride is the _____.

I also like _____ with my friends.

**10** Complete the questions. Then match.

like   dance   watch   play   go

**1** Will they _____ the chocolate cake?

**2** Will they _____ football tomorrow?

**3** Will they _____ to the aquarium?

**4** Will they _____ a funny film?

**5** Will they _____ at the school disco?

**a** I'm not sure. It might be raining.

**b** No, they won't. They like scary films.

**c** Yes, they will. They love watching the fish.

**d** Yes, they will. They really love music.

**e** I'm sure they will. They love sweet things.

**11**  **Listen and complete.**

shall   water park   much   else   could   where

**Louise:**   Hi, Pamela! ¹_____ we go out?

**Pamela:**   OK, ²_____ can we go?

**Louise:**   Shall we go to the ³_____?

**Pamela:**   I don't like swimming very ⁴_____. Where ⁵_____ could we go?

**Louise:**   If you like animals, we ⁶_____ go to the Natural History Museum?

**Pamela:**   Great! I haven't been there yet!

**12** **Read and match.**

**1**   What time shall we meet?

**2**   Where shall we have lunch?

**3**   Shall I open the window?

**4**   Shall we go to the cinema tonight?

**5**   I've left my lunch at home.

**a**   Yes, please. It's too warm!

**b**   What about ten o'clock?

**c**   I'm sorry but I'm having dinner with my grandparents.

**d**   You could buy a sandwich from the canteen.

**e**   There's a new restaurant by the university. Shall we try it?

**13** **Complete your own questions and sentences.**

**1**   I don't like swimming. What else _____?

**2**   It's hot and sunny. Shall we _____?

**3**   I don't like scary rides. We could _____.

**4**   She likes the theme park. She could _____.

**5**   I'm hungry! Shall we _____?

**6**   It's raining. We could _____.

**14** Read and tick (✓).

**1** Who was not happy in this part of the story?

a b c

**2** Who said that Dot and Zeb might have used the THD for power?

a b c

**15** Answer the questions.

**1** Did Matt and AL fly in the space pod?

_____

**2** Did Carol Carnival see a flash and hear a big bang?

_____

**3** Did Bella find the pod?

_____

**16**  Listen and number.

**a** water park ☐    **b** palace ☐

**c** aquarium ☐    **d** circus tent ☐

**17** **Think and write.**

6

**VALUES**

Learn to be self-sufficient. You can always do some things by yourself.

*Things I like to do by myself*

_____
_____
_____
_____
_____
_____
_____

*Things I like to do in a group*

_____
_____
_____
_____
_____

**18** **Read. Then sort and write the words with the correct prefix.**

**PHONICS & SPELLING**

~~possible~~  happy  visible  ~~tidy~~  like  cycle  order  heat  formal  fit
historic  credible  tell  regular  act  healthy  pay  personal  cook  legal
agree  appear  resistible  mature  usual  responsible  write  call  polite

| un– | dis– | im– | re– | pre– | i– | in– |
|-----|------|-----|-----|------|-----|-----|
| untidy | | impossible | | | | |

**19** **Complete the sentences.**  unfair  rewrite  disagree  preheat  irresponsible

**1** This rule is very _____.

**2** I _____ with you!

**3** It's _____ not to recycle.

**4** I have to _____ my presentation on wild animals.

**5** To cook this pizza you have to _____ the oven.

**20** **Look and write.**

barometer    thermometer    anemometer    humidity    pressure    satellite

1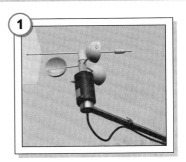

2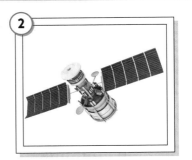

3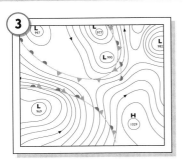

4

5

6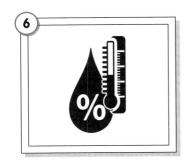

**21** **Read and circle.**

Meteorologists tell us what the [1] ( weather / clouds ) will be like. They use many different methods. [2] ( Rain / Clouds ) tell them if it will rain or if it will be sunny. Satellites send [3] ( weather reports / photos ) of the Earth to weather stations. Meteorologists also study air pressure systems. [4] ( High / Low ) pressure means it will rain soon. They also measure humidity to see how hot or cold we will feel. Weather balloons [5] ( take meteorologists to the sky / send information ) with a special radio signal. They've got anemometers to measure [6] ( wind pressure / temperature ) in them.

**22** **Write three interesting things you have learnt about the weather.**

_____

_____

_____

# Wider World

**(23)** Read the text about Debra's holiday. Tick (✓) the types of transport she used.

Last year we visited Greece. First, we took a plane from London to Athens, and then we took a boat to the island of Hydra. The journey from Athens only took us an hour and a half. Hydra is a beautiful, small island with friendly people. The one thing that is different about this island is that there are no cars or buses! The only form of transport are donkeys and bikes! Our 'taxi' to the hotel, which was at the top of the town, was a donkey. Because there were five of us, we had five donkeys! It was fun. At first, this was a little weird, but then I really enjoyed the peace and quiet! No noise or pollution from cars or buses. It was magic. – Debra, 12

☐ train   ☐ plane   ☐ boat   ☐ car   ☐ bus   ☐ donkey

**(24)** Look at Activity 23 and circle *T* (True) or *F* (False).

**1** The journey from London to Athens took one and a half hours.   T / F

**2** Hydra hasn't got cars or buses.   T / F

**3** Each member of Debra's family had their own donkey.   T / F

**4** Debra missed the cars and buses.   T / F

**(25)** Read and complete the graph.

John and I asked fifty pupils in my school how they travelled on their holidays last year. Here are the results of our survey.

- twenty-six travelled by car
- thirteen travelled by train
- eleven travelled by plane
- On their holiday, some pupils also travelled by:
  boat – eight
  bike – fifteen
  rickshaw – three

30
25
20
15
10
5
0

car

**26** Read and write.

> theme park    come    visited    jumped on the trampoline    will

Hi Elliot,

I'm having a great time! You ¹_____
love Adventure World when you come here! Yesterday we
²_____ the famous
³_____! In the evening, we went
rollerblading and then ⁴_____!
I don't think I want to ⁵_____ home!
How are your holidays?
I'll see you soon,
Cheers,
Sam

**27**  **Listen and circle.**

**1**    Oliver went to the ( water park / theme park ).

**2**    The rides were ( boring / exciting ).

**3**    The weather was ( rainy / sunny ).

**4**    Oliver went ( on the trampoline / rollerblading ).

## WRITING TIP!

We can use the past simple to talk about what we did, e.g.
*I/We was/were (in/at)...*
*I/We went... I/We saw...*

We can use *will* and *going to* to talk about our future plans and decisions, e.g.
*I think I will... We are going to...*

**28** **Imagine you went on a holiday to Adventure World. Complete the postcard.**

We went to _____.

On the first day, we _____.

Then _____.

After that, _____.

We had a great time!

**29** **Read and match.**

| | | | | |
|---|---|---|---|---|
| **1** | dodgems | **a** | You can go on boats here. |
| **2** | aquarium | **b** | You can sail in this but not on the sea. |
| **3** | boating lake | **c** | This is a big natural area in the mountains or forest. |
| **4** | roller coaster | **d** | Children can drive these. |
| **5** | circus | **e** | A king or queen lives here. |
| **6** | pirate ship | **f** | You can see many types of fish here. |
| **7** | national park | **g** | This is a fast and exciting ride but not wet. |
| **8** | palace | **h** | This is usually in a big tent. |

**30** **Read and number the conversation in order.**

**a** ☐ We could go to the aquarium.

**b** ☐ That's a good idea. We can ride around the new boating lake.

**c** ☐ Hi, Henry. What shall we do today?

**d** ☐ I'm not sure. It's already three o'clock and it closes at six o'clock.

**e** ☐ OK. See you soon!

**f** ☐ Yes, you're right. How about going to the park with our bikes?

**31** **Write two things you will do tomorrow and two things you won't do.**

_____

_____

**32** **Answer the questions for you.**

**1** What do you think you will do next summer?

_____

**2** How will you get there?

_____

**3** What do you think the weather will be like?

_____

**I CAN**

I can talk about future plans and intentions using *will*.

I can talk about attractions and make suggestions using *shall* and *could*.

I can write a postcard describing a holiday.

# 7 Space

## 1 Read and match. Then write.

1 tele
2 astro
3 space
4 space

a en
b et
c station
d met

5 pla
6 rock
7 ali
8 co
9 sate
10 space

e llite
f net
g naut
h scope
i ship
j shuttle

1   telescope     2 _____     3 _____

4 _____   5 _____     6 _____

7 _____   8 _____     9 _____

10 _____

## 2 Look, read and match.

SUN  Mercury  Earth  Jupiter  Uranus
Venus  Mars  Saturn  Neptune

1   What is the fourth planet from the Sun?        a   Jupiter

2   What is the third planet from the Sun?         b   Neptune

3   Which planet has got a lot of moons?           c   Mars

4   Which planet is the astronaut next to?         d   Earth

## 3 Complete the sentences.

1   _____ travel in space shuttles.

2   You can look at stars and planets through a _____.

3   _____ are creatures from another planet.

**4** Complete the sentences using the correct form of *should* or *need to*.

**1**  You _____ go to school every day.

**2**  They _____ learn about the solar system. It's very interesting.

**3**  She _____ see the new *Star Wars* film. She will like it.

**4**  You _____ call an ambulance. She doesn't feel well.

**5**  Plants _____ have water to live.

**6**  He _____ do his homework before he watches TV.

**5** Put the words in order to make sentences.

**1**  ought / try / you / to / astronaut's / food

_____

**2**  better / you'd / turn / off / TV / the

_____

**3**  he / astronomy / study / should

_____

**4**  doesn't / he / to / need / take / telescope / his

_____

**6** Read the answers and write the questions.

**1**  How often do you need to do your homework?

I need to do my homework every day.

**2**  _____ ?

They should try the new restaurant because it's amazing.

**3**  _____ ?

We'd better hurry up because we might be late.

**4**  _____ ?

It's our teacher who says we need to take more tests.

**7** Sort the words. Write them in the table.

| important | exciting | scary | frightening | tall | kind |
| intelligent | difficult | pretty | complicated | small | clever |

| One or two syllables [big / ea-sy] | Three syllables or more [a-ma-zing] |
|---|---|
|  |  |
|  |  |
|  |  |
|  |  |
|  |  |
|  |  |

**8** Read and tick (✓) if you agree or cross (✗) if you disagree.

**1**  Sci-fi films are more interesting than cartoons.  ☐

**2**  Football is more complicated than basketball.  ☐

**3**  Theme parks are more amazing than national parks.  ☐

**4**  Elephants are more frightening than tigers.  ☐

**5**  Maths is more important than English.  ☐

**9** Think and complete the sentences.

| amazing | complicated | interesting | expensive |

**1**  Looking at the stars can be _____.

**2**  Learning about the planets is very _____.

**3**  Buying an astronaut outfit may be quite _____.

**4**  Travelling to other planets is very _____.

**10** **Read and answer for you.**

**1**   Who do you think are more intelligent, astronauts or doctors?

_I think that astronauts are more intelligent than doctors._

**2**   Which are less exciting, theme parks or computer games?

_____

**3**   Which is more complicated, Science or Maths?

_____

**4**   Which is the least difficult, riding a bike or riding a horse?

_____

**5**   Which is more interesting, reading a book or watching a film?

_____

**6**   Which is more expensive, a car or a house?

_____

**11**  🎧 **Listen and write the price and weight.**

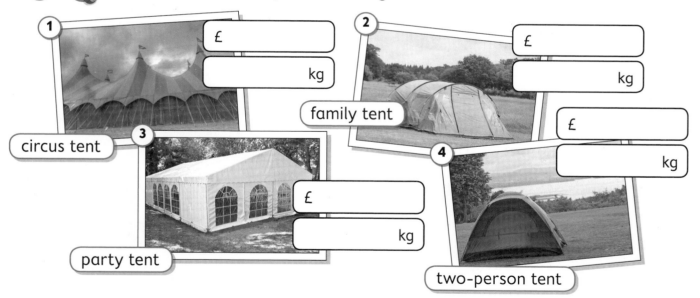

**1** £ _____  _____ kg

circus tent

**2** £ _____  _____ kg

family tent

**3** £ _____  _____ kg

party tent

**4** £ _____  _____ kg

two-person tent

**12** **Look at Activity 11 and answer the questions.**

**1**   Which is the most expensive tent?    _____

**2**   Which is the least expensive tent?    _____

**3**   Which tent weighs more, the party tent or the family tent?    _____

**13** Read and tick (✓).

**1**   Who thinks they see a comet?

**2**   Who can't wait to go home?

**14** Read and circle.

**1**   What are Zeb and Dot?

   **a** animals          **b** aliens          **c** astronauts

**2**   Dot and Zeb are happy because they found their ... .

   **a** planet.          **b** spaceship.          **c** machine.

**3**   What does Zeb use to start the machine?

   **a** his phone          **b** a computer          **c** the chip

**4**   What time of the day was it?

   **a** evening          **b** morning          **c** night

**15** Put the letters in the correct order to make words. Then write.

> dcixeet   inzagma   eplcaticdom   ilritblan

It's _____.

She's _____.

He's _____.

She says '_____.'

**16** Match and write. What materials can you use to make each model?

**VALUES**

Use your imagination to solve problems.

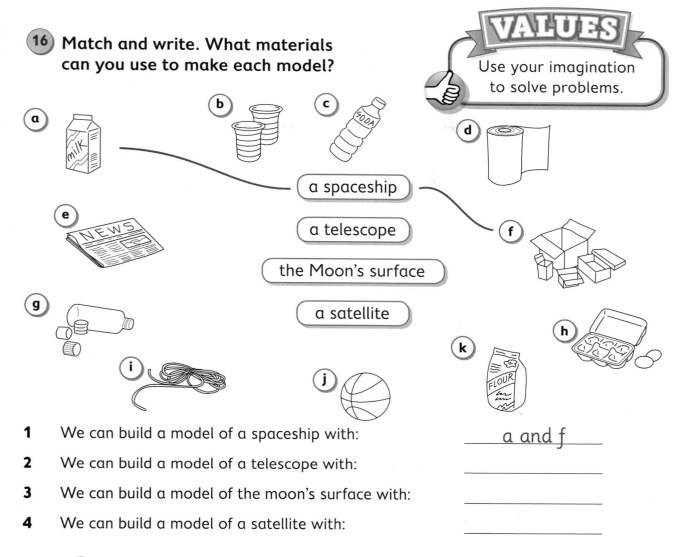

a spaceship

a telescope

the Moon's surface

a satellite

**1** We can build a model of a spaceship with:  _a and f_

**2** We can build a model of a telescope with:  _____

**3** We can build a model of the moon's surface with:  _____

**4** We can build a model of a satellite with:  _____

**17**  Listen and colour the sound.

**PHONICS & SPELLING**

| | | | | | |
|---|---|---|---|---|---|
| **1** | sm– | swam | smile | space | smell |
| **2** | sk– | street | skate | ski | Spain |
| **3** | sc– | surfing | sweet | screen | scarf |
| **4** | st– | stop | spider | storm | shop |
| **5** | sp– | spoon | speed | sky | story |

**18**  Listen and write.

| s– | | es– | |
|---|---|---|---|
| | | | |

**19** Read and complete.

plane   distorted   concave   convex   reflection

A mirror is a piece of glass that shows your ¹_____. There are different types of mirror and each one makes you look different. A 'normal' mirror is called a ²_____ mirror. A ³_____ mirror is a curved mirror which shows a ⁴_____ image and makes you look short and wide. A ⁵_____ mirror makes you look very tall and thin. You can find these two types of mirror in theme parks because they make you look funny!

**20** Read and experiment. Then complete the sentences.

long   distorted images   wide   short   thin

**Experiment with a spoon!**

Take a spoon and look at the reflection of your face on both sides. Are both images the same?

Explain.

**1**   Curved mirrors reflect _____.

**2**   In a convex mirror, I look _____

_____.

**3**   In a concave mirror, I look _____

_____.

**21** Read and answer.

**1**   Why does a driver have to be careful when they use a convex mirror?

_____

_____

**2**   What may happen to people who stand too far away from concave mirrors?

_____

_____

# Wider World

**22** **Read and circle.**

The nearest star to Earth is the [1]( Moon / Sun ). The colour of a star depends on
[2]( its temperature / how big it is ). Small, cooler stars are [3]( blue / red ), but big, heavy
stars are almost [4]( red / blue ) and very hot. The first man in space was
[5]( Neil Armstrong / Yuri Gagarin ) in 1961. He spent almost two hours in space.
[6]( Neil Armstrong / Yuri Gagarin ) was the first man to walk on the Moon in 1969. Mars
is Earth's neighbour. It has got polar ice caps like [7]( the Moon / Earth ) and they are
made of frozen water. It has also got volcanoes. Earth has got a [8]( shorter / longer )
year than Mars. Scientists believe that there could have been life on Mars in the past!

**23** **Can you remember the planets? Look at this phrase to help you.**

**My Very Excellent Mother Just Served Us Noodles**

Mercury Venus Earth Mars Jupiter Saturn Uranus Neptune

**24** **Now write a new phrase to help you remember the planets.**

M _____  V _____  E _____  M _____

J _____  S _____  U _____  N _____

**25** **Read and write B (Beginning) or E (Ending).**

**1** In the end, we all sat around the campfire and told our stories. We had a great time and were relieved that there was no bear in the forest after all! ____

**2** One hot day last summer, we decided to go swimming. We packed a picnic basket, put on sun cream and hats and got into the car. ____

**3** On my way to school one morning, I saw Pedro running towards the park. I called out to him but he didn't stop. I decided to follow him. ____

**4** This story has a happy ending because we found our money and passports. After a lot of adventures, we were able to get on our plane and start our holiday. ____

**26** **Look at Activity 25. What do we put in an opening paragraph? Tick (✓).**

**1** where ☐          **2** how it all started ☐

**3** how it ended ☐          **4** what happened in the middle of the story ☐

**5** when ☐          **6** who is in the story ☐

**27** **Look at Activity 26. What do we put in our closing paragraph? Write.**

_____

_____

_____

_____

> **WRITING TIP!**
>
> Beginning a story:
> *Last summer...*
> *It all began a few weeks ago...*
> *One cold winter morning...*
>
> Ending a story:
> *It all ended when...*
> *Late that night...*
> *When I woke up I realised...*

**28** **Write a different ending for Connor's story.**

'Jake. Jake,' said someone softly. _____

_____

_____

**29** Write the correct words.

> intelligent   complicated   fascinatinga telescope   frightening   comet

**1** very interesting _____
**2** difficult to understand _____
**3** this is bright and has a tail _____
**4** clever _____
**5** you use this to see stars and planets _____
**6** scary _____

**30** Complete.   important   most   horrible   least   more   second   amazing   less

I want to buy some new trainers. I've seen three different pairs. The first pair are green with
rockets on. They're ¹_____ but they're the ²_____ expensive at £105.
The ³_____ pair are ⁴_____ expensive. They look OK, but the first pair are
⁵_____ beautiful. This pair cost £75. The last pair are the ⁶_____ expensive at
£20, but they look ⁷_____. My mum says price is the most ⁸_____ thing!

**31** Read and give advice.

**1** Pedro wants to go outside, but it's very cold.

_____

**2** Maria and Emma have got a lot of homework, but they are still watching TV.

_____

**3** Lena talks too much on the phone and doesn't do her homework.

_____

**32** Put the words in order to make questions. Then write answers.

**1** intelligent / whales / are / which / less / dogs / or
<u>Which are less intelligent, whales or dogs?</u>   _____

**2** planet / which / most / the / interesting / is
_____ ?   _____

**I·CAN**

I can give advice using *should*, *ought to*, *had better* and *need to*.  ☐ ☐ ☐

I can make comparisons using opinion adjectives and *more*,
*the most*, *less (than)* and *the least*.  ☐ ☐ ☐

I can write a short story.  ☐ ☐ ☐

# 8 The environment

**1** Write.  paper  recycle  turn off  reuse  use  rubbish  shower  batteries

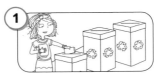
1 recycle _____

2 collect _____

3 _____ bottles

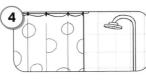
4 take a _____

5 _____ plastic bags

6 _____ public transport

7 _____ the lights

8 recharge _____

**2** Look at the chart and complete.

Do you reuse plastic bags?

1 ___Five___ people always reuse plastic bags.

2 _____ people sometimes reuse plastic bags.

3 _____ people usually reuse plastic bags.

4 _____ people never reuse plastic bags.

5 The total number of people in the survey was _____.

**3** Write about yourself.

How often do you:

1 recycle paper? _____

2 recharge batteries? _____

3 collect rubbish? _____

4 turn off the lights? _____

5 use public transport? _____

6 reuse plastic bags? _____

**4** Look and write.

| a glass   no   a bottle (x2)   a little   half   a few |

1 _____ vinegar

2 _____ of juice

3 _____ salt

4 _____ a glass of water

5 _____ of cola

6 _____ cake

7 _____ bananas

**5** Read and circle.

1 Mum needs ( enough / plenty ) of rest after working all day.

2 We should buy cleaners that have ( no / enough ) chemicals in them.

3 There is ( a few / a little ) water in the bottle.

4 We have ( a few / a little ) old toys for the charity event.

5 I haven't got ( no / enough ) money for a new computer game.

**6** Tick (✓) the correct sentences. Then correct the incorrect ones.

1 There's a few water to make a natural cleaner. ☐

_____

2 There is enough sugar to make a cake. ☐

_____

3 Do you need a few help with your homework? ☐

_____

4 There is no bread on the table! ☐

_____

**7** **Read and match.**

1    What can you do to save trees?

2    What can you do to conserve energy?

3    What can you do to save resources?

4    What can you do to keep the planet clean?

a    Collect rubbish.

b    Recycle bottles.

c    Recycle paper.

d    Turn off the lights.

**8** **Read, think and sort. One word can go in two circles.**

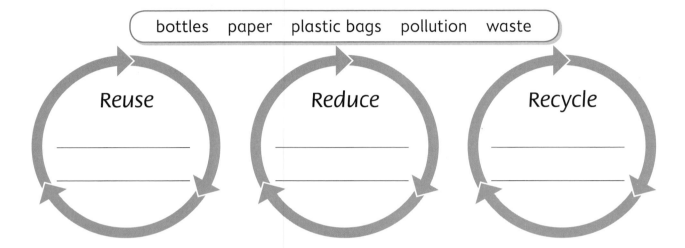

bottles   paper   plastic bags   pollution   waste

Reuse

_____

_____

Reduce

_____

_____

Recycle

_____

_____

**9** **Look and write sentences.**

1    <u>We cut down too many trees. We should</u> _____ .

2    _____

3    _____

**10** **What can you do to save the Earth? Write a green diary for next week.**

I'm going to _____

_____

_____

**11**  **Listen and number.**

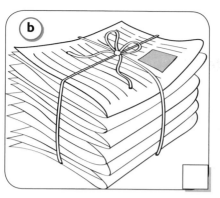

**12** **Look at Activity 11 and complete the sentences.**

**a** If you __recycle bottles__ , you'll __save resources__ .

**b** If you _____, you'll _____.

**c** If you _____, you'll _____.

**d** If you _____, you'll _____.

**e** If you _____, you'll _____.

**f** If you _____, you'll _____.

**13** **Complete the sentences.**

**1** If you use solar energy (from the Sun), _____.

**2** You will reduce pollution if _____.

**3** If you cycle every day, _____.

**4** It will help my local community if I _____.

**5** If I reuse paper at school, _____.

**14** **Read and tick (✓).**

**1** Who did AL give the chip to?

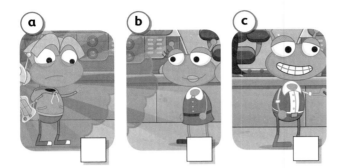

**2** What did Dot and Zeb use to send a message to their people?

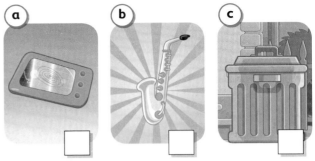

**15**  **Listen and match.**

**1** 'Did they go home in the end?'

**2** 'I've got some news for you both.'

**3** 'What? That's frightening!'

**4** 'They were aliens from Mars.'

**16** **Circle or write your own answer.**

**1** I think Bella is...
  **a** brilliant.
  **b** intelligent.
  **c** _____.

**2** I think the THD is...
  **a** amazing.
  **b** complicated.
  **c** _____.

**3** My favourite character is...
  **a** Matt.
  **b** Dot.
  **c** _____.

**4** I think the story was...
  **a** interesting.
  **b** fascinating.
  **c** _____.

**17** Which items do you use every day? Tick (✓) then write the words in the diagram.

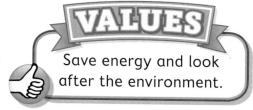

VALUES

Save energy and look after the environment.

| 1 | water | ☐ | 2 | food cans | ☐ |
| 3 | electricity | ☐ | 4 | wrapping paper | ☐ |
| 5 | plastic cups | ☐ | 6 | plastic bags | ☐ |
| 7 | juice cartons | ☐ | 8 | cardboard boxes | ☐ |
| 9 | writing paper | ☐ | 10 | glass bottles | ☐ |

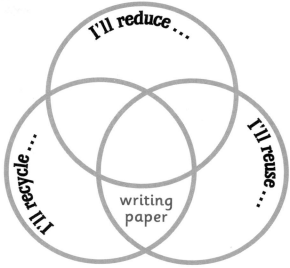

I'll reduce...

I'll recycle...

I'll reuse...

writing paper

PHONICS & SPELLING

**18** Read and circle *–sion* in red and *–tion* in blue.

1 Communication and information are very important in the twenty-first century.

2 The country is in an economic recession.

3 The reduction of pollution is necessary in our cities.

4 Pupils need motivation and action in their lessons.

5 It is difficult to make a decision in this situation.

6 Yesterday I watched a science fiction film.

7 There was a terrible explosion.

8 This investigation is very interesting.

**19** Write four sentences. Use *–sion* and *–tion* words from Activity 18.

1 _____

2 _____

3 _____

4 _____

**20** **Read and circle.**

**1**   Many animal and insect ( species / crops ) are in danger.

**2**   Bees ( pollinate / survive ) flowers and produce honey.

**3**   The farmer's ( wax / crop ) was destroyed after the heavy rains.

**4**   Bees live in ( colonies / species ) with thousands of other bees.

**5**   It's difficult for animals to ( pollinate / survive ) if we don't protect them.

**21** **Read the text on Pupil's Book page 94 again. Then read and match.**

| | | | |
|---|---|---|---|
| **1** | 25,000 | **a** | species of flowers that need bees |
| **2** | million of years | **b** | different types of bees |
| **3** | more than seventy | **c** | bees have lived on Earth |
| **4** | 250,000 | **d** | kilograms of honey that a colony can produce |
| **5** | fourteen | **e** | food bees pollinate |

**22** **Correct the sentences.**

**1**   All species of bees can produce honey.

_____

**2**   Seeds make pollen which become flowers or fruit.

_____

**3**   Insects and birds can survive without flowers.

_____

**4**   We need bats, frogs and lizards to help bees.

_____

**23** **Write two things you found interesting about bees.**

_____
_____

# Wider World

**24** **Read and match.**

| | |
|---|---|
| **1** Air pollution | **a** in floods. |
| **2** We need cleaner sources of energy | **b** animals to die. |
| **3** Animals lose their habitats | **c** is poisonous gases in the air. |
| **4** Droughts cause | **d** billions of tonnes of rubbish. |
| **5** Humans produce | **e** kills many ocean animals. |
| **6** Rubbish in our rivers and seas | **f** to keep the air we breathe clean. |

**25** **Tick (✓) the ways we can protect the environment.**

**1** use energy from the sun ☐

**2** turn on the lights in the day ☐

**3** plant more trees ☐

**4** use rechargeable batteries in our cars ☐

**5** take long, hot baths ☐

**6** recycle as many things as we can ☐

**7** increase the amount of plastic we use ☐

**8** cut down trees to make furniture ☐

**26** **Look at Activity 25. Write three ways we can protect the environment.**

**1** If we turn on the lights in the day, we will use too much energy.

**2** _____

**3** _____

**27** **Complete the instructions.**

> Make three ropes long enough for someone to skip with.
> Wrap the tape around the rope a few times to make handles.
> Cut the rectangles into strips.

## How to *make a skipping rope* with *plastic bags.*

**Materials:**

- plastic bags
- scissors
- tape

**Instructions:**

**1** Cut plastic bags open and cut off the handles.

**2** Cut the pieces of plastic you have into rectangles.

**3** 1 _____

**4** Tie the ends of the strips together until you make a long rope.

**5** 2 _____

**6** Braid the three ropes together.

**7** 3 _____

**8** Start skipping!

**WRITING TIP!**

For instructions, we can use imperative verbs, e.g. *mix, stir, put, add.*

**28** **Choose an idea. Then write instructions for how to make it.**

- A tin-can pencil holder
- A plastic-bottle flower pot
- A plastic-bag kite

_____

_____

_____

_____

_____

_____

**29** **Read and match.**

1 conserve
2 reduce
3 pollution
4 public transport
5 energy

a poison in the environment
b light is an example of this
c save or keep
d make less
e a train is an example of this

**30** **Read and circle.**

I'm going to help make my school greener. My friends and I are going to put ¹( recycling / plastic ) boxes in every classroom. Then we can ²( pick up / turn off ) paper and ³( transport / bottles ) to recycle. My family is also going to help ⁴( reduce / save ) the planet at home. We're going to ⁵( use / turn off ) the lights when we go outside, and my mum is going to ⁶( use / reuse ) public transport to go to the supermarket.

**31** **Put the words in order. Then match to make sentences.**

1 public / transport / if / you / use

_____,

2 pick up / if / rubbish / you

_____,

3 you / recycle / if / paper

_____,

4 the / off / lights / if / you / turn

_____,

a you'll conserve energy.

b you'll reduce pollution.

c you'll save trees.

d you'll keep the planet clean.

**32** **Tick (✓) the correct sentences. Correct the incorrect ones in your notebook.**

1 There is enough food for everyone here. ☐
2 There are a little bags on the floor. ☐
3 There is a few water in the glass. ☐
4 We have plenty of time to walk home. ☐

**I-CAN**

I can talk about ways to help the environment, using *a little*, *a few*, *plenty (of)*, *no* and *enough*.

I can talk about the consequences of protecting the environment, using the first conditional.

I can write instructions for how to do something.

**1** 🎧 **Listen and circle *T* (True) or *F* (False).**

3:45

**a** Matt's boss wanted to know where the new THD was.　　T / F

**b** Matt and AL will go back to work.　　T / F

**c** Zeb and Dot had a long journey home.　　T / F

**d** They enjoyed their time on Earth.　　T / F

**e** Bella didn't have to do her chores.　　T / F

**f** She'll tell her friends about her adventures.　　T / F

**2** **Look at the pictures and answer the questions.**

**1** Whose is this?　　_____

**2** What did they use it for?　　_____

**3** Who made this music?　　_____

**4** Why was it important?　　_____

**5** Whose is this?　　_____

**6** Where were they when they used it?　　_____

**3** **Answer the questions. Write *Yes, he/she/they/it did* or *No, he/she/they/it didn't*.**

**1** Did the THD work after Bella looked at it?　　_____

**2** Was Bella good at helping Matt and AL?　　_____

**3** Was Matt angry at the end of the story?　　_____

**4** Was getting the new THD back important to AL?　　_____

**5** Did the Martins keep the new THD?　　_____

**6** Did Dot and Zeb go home to Mars?　　_____

## 4 Read and circle. Then write.

**1**     Deforestation is when you ( plant / cut down ) trees.
Write two reasons why we should save our forests.

_____

_____

**2**     Fossils are found in ( zoos / rocks ).
What do we learn from fossils?

_____

_____

**3**     You can present numbers in a bar ( table / graph ).
What kind of things can you present in a graph?

_____

_____

**4**     Physical activities help you keep ( healthy / unhealthy ).
What do you do to keep healthy?

_____

_____

**5**     Reggae, pop and rock are all types of ( music / instruments ).
Which is your favourite instrument? Why?

_____

_____

**6**     Weather reports help prevent ( storms / accidents at sea ).
Describe one method used to predict the weather.

_____

_____

**7**     Convex is a word we use to describe ( Science / mirrors ).
What does a convex mirror make you look like?

_____

_____

**8**     Bees are responsible for the ( survival / species ) of many plants and animals.
How do bees help the planet?

_____

_____

**5** Write about you.

**My past**

1 Last summer, I _____ .

2 Yesterday, I _____ by myself.

3 I've never _____ .

**My present**

4 I'm good at _____ .

5 I like _____ , but I don't like _____ .

6 I love _____ and _____ .

7 I can _____ , but I can't _____ .

8 There is a _____ my home.

9 I want to _____ .

10 I have to _____ .

**My future**

11 Tomorrow when I get up, first I _____ .

12 Then I _____ .

13 Next year, I _____ .

14 If I study hard at school, I _____ .

**6** Draw three animals. Then write about them.

| | | |
|---|---|---|
| | | |

1 The _____ is taller than the _____ .

2 The _____ is the _____ .

3 The _____ .

4 The _____ .

**7** Complete the questions. Then ask and answer.

how   what   when   where   which   who   why

1 _____ are you happy?

2 _____ is that bright light?

3 _____ is the most frightening?

4 _____ is your favourite film star?

5 _____ do you live?

6 _____ do you get up?

7 _____ did you get here?

**8** Make a poster about how to help the environment. Then write.

1 We should _____.

2 We need to _____.

3 We ought to _____.

4 If we _____, we'll _____.

3 I'm going to _____.

# Bonfire Night

**1** **Look and match.**

  **a**

  **b**

  **c**

  **d**

**1**    James I was the King of England. ☐    **2**    Guy Fawkes. He didn't like the King. ☐

**3**    The Houses of Parliament, London. ☐    **4**    The guards. ☐

**2**  **Listen. Then number the sentences.**

## How Guy Fawkes' plan failed

☐ On November the 5th, guards found Guy Fawkes in the basement. The King and the Houses of Parliament were safe!

☐ Guy and his friends knew about explosives. They wanted to put gunpowder in barrels in the basement of the Houses of Parliament on November the 5th, 1605.

☐ In 1603, James I became the new King of England. Not everybody in England liked him.

☐ The King received an anonymous letter about the plot.

☐ A man called Guy Fawkes and his friends wanted to blow up the Houses of Parliament with the King inside.

**3** **Read and match.**

**1**    When do they celebrate Bonfire Night in the UK and why?

**2**    What do people do on Bonfire Night?

**a**    People have bonfires and they watch fireworks. It's fun!

**b**    Bonfire Night takes place every year on the 5th of November to celebrate how Guy Fawkes' plan failed.

**4** **Answer the questions.**

**1**    When do people have bonfires and fireworks? _____

**2**    What are people celebrating? _____

# Christmas crackers

**1** **Read the text on Pupil's Book page 105 again and answer the questions.**

**1** Who invented the Christmas cracker? _____

**2** What is a Christmas cracker? _____

**3** How does a Christmas cracker snap? _____

**4** What can you find inside a Christmas cracker? _____

**2** **Read and number the instructions in order.**

**a** Get some Christmas wrapping paper. ☐

**b** Put the note, joke and small gift inside. ☐

**c** Tie both ends. ☐

**d** Your Christmas cracker is ready to pull! ☐

**e** Make a small gift for your friend. ☐

**f** Write a joke. ☐

**g** Save a toilet paper roll from home. 1

**h** Cover the roll with the wrapping paper. ☐

**3** **Write a joke for your Christmas cracker.**

# Easter eggs

**1** 🎧 3:50 **Listen and number.**

**a** Egg decorating ☐

**b** Egg rolling ☐

**c** Egg hunt ☐

**d** Egg presents ☐

**2** **Read the instructions. Write *Yes* or *No*.**

*How to make Sticker Easter Eggs*

**1** Fill a swimming pool ½ to ¾ full of milk. _____

**2** Add a tablespoon of vinegar. _____

**3** Add some pencils until you like the colour! _____

**4** Put the stickers on the eggs. _____

**5** Let it boil for fifteen days. _____

**6** Remove from heat. _____

**7** Remove the eggs and keep them wet. _____

**8** Leave the stickers on the eggs. _____

**3** **Think of a dish made with hard-boiled eggs. Draw your dish. Write the recipe.**

## 1 Read and complete.

| 1877 | London | summer | July | player | then |

Every summer, a traditional tennis event takes place in ¹_____ in the last week of June and the first week of ²_____. Perhaps you have seen a tennis ³_____ from your country playing on the Wimbledon grass. The first championship took place in ⁴_____. Since ⁵_____, Wimbledon has been part of British ⁶_____ entertainment.

## 2 Read and circle T (True) or F (False).

1   A lot of people wait in a queue to spend a day at Wimbledon.     T / F

2   Tennis players always wear white.     T / F

3   People have strawberries with cream.     T / F

4   Wimbledon is not on TV.     T / F

## 3 🎧 Complete the sentences. Then listen and check.

| taxi | underground | bus | train |

1   If you get the _____, the nearest stop to the grounds is Southfields station.

2   If you go on to Waterloo station, you can get a _____ to Wimbledon station.

3   If you take _____ number 493 from Richmond, it will go directly to the grounds.

4   You can always get a _____ to Wimbledon if you are in London.

# Extra Practice

## Welcome

**1** Put the letters in order to make words.

**1** kscyip _____

**2** tecu _____

**3** thsmoo _____

**4** ietqu _____

**5** rndou _____

**6** dulo _____

**2** Read the answers and write the questions.

**1** _____ ?

It looks scary and wild.

**2** _____ ?

Yes, it looks good.

**3** _____ ?

No, it doesn't look scary.

**4** _____ ?

It feels soft and furry.

**5** _____ ?

It smells sweet.

**3** Write the correct words.

> ball   banana   monster   cat   baby

**1** It's small and cute. It's furry. _____

**2** It's round and hard. You play with it. _____

**3** It can be big or small. It's scary and sometimes furry. It can be loud. _____

**4** It's small and cute. _____

**5** It's long and soft. It's sweet. _____

# Unit 1

**1** **Read and circle.**

1    The children enjoy ( to swim / swimming ).

2    They ( start / starting ) working at 6 a.m.

3    We don't like ( visit / visiting ) museums.

4    They finish ( cooking / to cook ) at 8 p.m.

**2** **Read and circle.**

1    I'm hungry, ( but / so ) I'm making a sandwich.

2    I can't skate, ( but / so ) I can swim.

3    I can speak Chinese, ( but / so ) I'm going to China.

4    I am tired, ( but / so ) I'm going to bed early.

5    We can watch a film, ( but / so ) we mustn't stay up too late.

**3** **Read and match.**

| | | | |
|---|---|---|---|
| 1 | They're lighting a fire | **a** | to stop the tent falling down. |
| 2 | We need a compass | **b** | to see in the dark. |
| 3 | We're putting in the pegs | **c** | to keep warm. |
| 4 | I cover my head | **d** | to stay dry. |
| 5 | She needs a torch | **e** | to give us our direction. |

**4** **Write the correct words.**

> air mattress   air pump   rucksack   tent   first aid kit

1    You put everything you need to go camping inside this.    _____

2    A box with medicine.    _____

3    You sleep in this when you go camping.    _____

4    You sleep on this.    _____

5    We use this to blow up things.    _____

# Unit 2

**(1) Complete the sentences.**

**1** Giraffes are _____ (tall) than camels.

**2** Turtles are the _____ (slow) animals in the sea.

**3** Tigers are _____ (fast) than monkeys.

**4** Lemurs are _____ (small) animals in this zoo.

**(2) Put the words in order to make questions. Then write answers.**

**1** bigger / seals / otters / are / than

_____ ? _____

**2** cheetahs / faster / were / than / the / the / turtles

_____ ? _____

**3** the / is / lightest / the / animal / koala

_____ ? _____

**(3) Rewrite the sentences.**

**1** Scientists rescue animals in wild parks.

_____ are rescued by _____ in wild parks.

**2** People find fossils in rocks.

_____ are found _____ in rocks.

**3** People plant trees in forests.

_____

**(4) Read and match.**

| | | | | |
|---|---|---|---|---|
| **1** | A group of large reptiles that lived millions of years ago. | | **a** | butterfly |
| **2** | An animal with orange and black stripes. | | **b** | extinct |
| **3** | An insect with wings and beautiful colours. | | **c** | tiger |
| **4** | The shape or prints of extinct animals in rock. | | **d** | fossil |
| **5** | Doesn't exist now. | | **e** | dinosaurs |

# Unit 3

**(1) Write the correct words.**

front   end   straight   next   between   corner

How do you get to the supermarket?

Go ¹_____ ahead.
Turn right at the ²_____. At the ³_____ of the road
turn left ⁴_____ to the chemist. Walk another five hundred metres and
the supermarket is in ⁵_____ of you. It's ⁶_____
the post office and the bookshop.

**(2) Read and match.**

1   If you want to go to university,          **a**   you can buy them at the post office.

2   If you wait at the bus stop,              **b**   you should ring to make a reservation.

3   If you want to stay at the guest house,   **c**   you can see when the next bus will arrive.

4   If you use the underground,               **d**   you can get to school quicker.

5   If you need some stamps,                  **e**   you should study hard.

**(3) Complete the sentences using *as ... as*.**

1   We haven't got _____ pets _____ my friend has got.

2   There are _____ bus stops on this street _____ on that street.

3   There isn't _____ information on this website _____ I need.

4   I don't drink _____ water _____ I should.

5   He received _____ presents _____ his sister.

**(4) Write the correct words.**

university   theatre   stadium   underground   factory

1   A place where people can see a play.                          _____

2   A system of trains running under a city.                      _____

3   A large building with no roof where you can see a sport.      _____

4   A place where people study for a degree.                      _____

5   A building where people make things with machines.           _____

# Unit 4

**1** **Read and find the mistakes. Then write correct sentences.**

**1** I maked a pizza last night. _____

**2** We eated a nice big salad for dinner. _____

**3** The chef cookt a nice meal. _____

**4** I haved a sandwich for lunch. _____

**2** **Complete the sentences with the correct form of the verb.**

**1** Yesterday my dad cooked fish and chips while I _____ (watch) TV.

**2** They _____ (wait) for two hours, but he never came.

**3** What _____ (she / do) at seven o'clock last night?

**4** You _____ (not / study) when we called.

**3** **Complete the questions.**

**1** You had dinner at home, _____?

**2** She didn't see the new film, _____?

**3** They sat by the window, _____?

**4** Mark didn't sleep well last night, _____?

**4** **Write the correct words.**

ingredients   omelette   recipe   oven   paella   list   curry

**1** You turn it on and put food in it to cook. _____

**2** You read this to find out how to make a certain food. _____

**3** These are what we use to make a meal. _____

**4** You make this to remind you what you need to buy. _____

**5** A spicy dish. _____

**6** A dish with rice and seafood, vegetables or meat. _____

**7** A dish made with eggs. _____

# Unit 5

**(1) Read and find the mistakes. Then write correct sentences.**

**1**   Have you never seen a whale? _____

**2**   We haven't opened the box already. _____

**3**   They have yet finished their homework. _____

**4**   I have been to a concert just. _____

**(2) Complete the sentences.**   [ since   for   yet   already ]

**1**   I've lived here _____ three years.

**2**   She's learnt many things _____ she started to read.

**3**   We haven't been to that restaurant _____.

**4**   Have you _____ practised for the concert?

**(3) Read and match.**

**1**   I have been a fan of thrillers since          **a**   on holiday yet.

**2**   He has already had                             **b**   his birthday.

**3**   We have liked classical music for             **c**   about a year.

**4**   They haven't been                              **d**   I was ten.

**5**   You have just seen a play which               **e**   finished five minutes ago.

**(4) Write the correct words.**

[ triangle   comedy   cymbal   biography   rap ]

**1**   It's a film that makes you laugh.                                              _____

**2**   It's a type of modern music where musicians talk rather than sing.           _____

**3**   A musician bangs two together to make a loud sound.                          _____

**4**   It's a film that is based on true life.                                       _____

**5**   This musical instrument is also a shape.                                      _____

# Unit 6

**1** **Answer these questions about next weekend. Then write.**

**1** What will you do?   **2** What will your sister/brother do?

**3** What will your parents do?   **4** What will your family do together?

Next weekend, _____

_____

_____

_____

**2** **Read the answers and write the questions using _Shall_ or _What else_.**

**1** _Shall we go to the cinema?_   Yes, I'd love to go to the cinema.

**2** _____? We could go to the castle after we eat lunch.

**3** _____? Maybe not. I've seen the pyramids before.

**4** _____? What about making a snowman after we ski?

**3** **Complete the sentences with _will_ or _going to_.**

**1** The sky is dark. It _____ snow.

**2** The baby's face is red. She _____ cry.

**3** This _____ be the best party ever.

**4** You _____ be very successful in your new job.

**4** **Write the correct words.**

mini-golf   skyscraper   carousel   boating lake   water park

**1** A very tall building in a city. _____

**2** You can row a boat here. _____

**3** You can swim and go on water slides here. _____

**4** It's a game where you hit a ball into holes in the ground. _____

**5** You sit on horses which go up and down, and round and round. _____

# Unit 7

**(1) Read and circle.**

1   You ( shouldn't / need to ) watch so much TV.

2   He ( needn't / should ) clean his room. I'll do it.

3   She ( ought to / will ) learn about stars. It's fun!

4   ( Shouldn't / Ought to ) we turn off the lights to see the stars?

5   We'd ( better / should ) go or we will miss the bus.

**(2) Read and think. Do you agree? Tick (✓) or cross (✗).**

1   Science is less complicated than Maths.

2   Earth is the least interesting planet.

3   Being an astronaut is more dangerous than being a teacher.

4   Flying is more expensive than taking a train.

5   Learning is the most important thing at school.

**(3) Read and circle.**

1   You ( may / has / ought ) be right.

2   Visitors ( had / may / mustn't ) only enter one at a time.

3   She ( will / might / must ) go to the party. She's not too sure.

4   I ( have / might / must ) pass the test. I knew most of the answers.

**(4) Read and match.**

1   A living being from another planet.                          **a**   space shuttle

2   You use this to look at the stars and planets.               **b**   planet

3   This can help meteorologists predict the weather.            **c**   satellite

4   Earth is one of these.                                       **d**   alien

5   Something that can take you to the moon.                     **e**   telescope

# Unit 8

**(1) Complete the sentences.**

[ no    a little    plenty    a few    enough ]

**1** There isn't _____ food for all these people.

**2** There's _____ paper in the cupboard – we need to order more!

**3** I have _____ time before the test.

**4** There are _____ people here today.

**5** She's got _____ of clothes to choose from.

**(2) Complete the sentences.**

**1** If you save trees, _____.

**2** You will conserve energy if you _____.

**3** If you pick up rubbish, _____.

**4** _____ if you use public transport.

**(3) Complete the questions using *How much* or *How many*. Then write answers.**

**1** _____ children are there in your class?

_____

**2** _____ paper do you recycle?

_____

**3** _____ plastic bottles do you use a week?

_____

**4** _____ electricity do you use?

_____

**(4) Read and match.**

**1** to make a gift (normally to a charity)        **a** conserve

**2** to save (natural resources, like water, wood etc.)        **b** donate

**3** use again        **c** reduce

**4** use less of        **d** reuse

# Picture Dictionary

## Unit 1 Adventure camp

### Camping equipment

 sleeping bag

 tent

 rucksack

 pegs

 compass

 torch

 campsite

 fire

 first aid kit

 air pump

 air mattress

### Camping activities

 take down the tent

 pitch the tent

 put in the pegs

 set up the bed

 cover our heads

 light a fire

 keep out of the rain

 read a compass

### Deforestation

 conserving

 dense

 drought

 humid

 deforestation

# Unit 2  Wildlife park

## Wild animals

rhino

cheetah

koala

lemur

camel

whale

seal

otter

turtle

tiger

## Superlative adjectives to describe animals

tallest

longest

shortest

biggest

smallest

heaviest

lightest

fastest

slowest

## Fossils

dinosaur

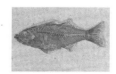
fossils

structure

extinct

palaeontologists

# Unit 3  Where we live

## Places in our town

shopping centre

post office

cinema

chemist

newsagent

college

circus

factory

theatre

supermarket

university

airport

bookshop

fire station

police station

railway station

bus stop

guest house

stadium

underground

## Urban and rural life

dirty

village

urban

rural

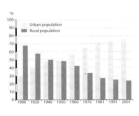
population

traffic

# Unit 4  Good food, good mood

## International food

curry

omelette

spaghetti

fish and chips

paella

dumplings

sushi

stew

rice and beans

## Cooking verbs and objects

made a list

bought food

read a recipe

prepared the ingredients

turned on the oven

served a meal

washed the dishes

had a meal

## Healthy lifestyles

balanced

lifestyle

physical exercise

energy

portions

# Unit 5 Arts and entertainment

## Film genres

thriller

comedy

sci-fi

romance

musical

cartoon

action

fantasy

biography

mystery

## Musical instruments

cello

harmonica

saxophone

triangle

cymbal

drums

clarinet

harp

tambourine

trumpet

## Types of music

rock

blues

country

pop

reggae

# Unit 6  Trips

## Tourist attractions

museum

aquarium

theme park

palace

botanical gardens

water park

castle

national park

skyscraper

## Theme park attractions

go on the big wheel

go on the dodgems

play mini-golf

go on the carousel

go on the boating lake

go on the rollercoaster

go on the pirate ship

go on the water slide

## Weather forecasting

barometer

thermometer

anemometer

humidity

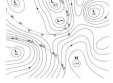
pressure

satellite

# Unit 7 Space

## Objects in space

space station

satellite

astronaut

planet

telescope

alien

spaceship

comet

space shuttle

rocket

## Opinion adjectives

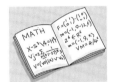

complicated

amazing

frightening

intelligent

brilliant

important

interesting

expensive

horrible

fascinating

## Distorting mirrors

concave

convex

reflection

distorted image

plane mirror

# Unit 8  The environment

## Ways to help the environment

recycle paper

recycle bottles

collect rubbish

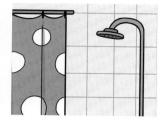
take a shower

reuse plastic bags

turn off the lights

use public
transport

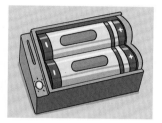
use rechargeable
batteries

## Ways to protect the environment

save trees

save resources

keep the
planet clean

donate food

reduce waste

conserve energy

reduce pollution

car pool

## Why we need bees

species

crop

colony

pollinate

survive

wax

**Pearson Education Limited**
KAO Two
KAO Park
Harlow
Essex CM17 9NA
England
and Associated Companies throughout the world.

Poptropica® English Islands

© Pearson Education Limited 2018

Editorial and project management by hyphen

First published 2018
ISBN: 978-1-292-19885-9

Set in Fiendstar 16/21pt
Printed in Neografia, Slovakia

**Acknowledgements:** The publisher would like to thank Catherine Zgouras, Magdalena Custodio and Oscar Ruiz for their contributions to this edition.

**Illustrators:** Charlotte Alder (The Bright Agency), Fred Blunt, Moreno Chiacchiera (Beehive Illustration), Lawrence Christmas, Leo Cultura, Mark Draisey, HL Studios, Sue King (Plum Pudding Illustration), John Martz, Simone Massoni (Advocate Art), Rob McClurkan (Beehive Illustration), Ken Mok, Olimpia Wong, Christos Skaltsas (hyphen)

**Picture Credits**
The publisher would like to thank the following for their kind permission to reproduce their photographs:

(Key: b-bottom; c-centre; l-left; r-right; t-top)

**123RF.com:** 13, 104 (compass), 109 (palace), 110 (alien), 110 (spaceship), cookelma 110 (astronaut), 110 (satellite), forplayday 110 (space shuttle), fotointeractiva 108 (saxophone), gavran333 69/3, kessudap 69/4, Paul Maguire 69/2, pilens 22br, 105 (fossils), sssccc 110 (telescope), Maksym Topchii 15l, vlue 108 (cymbal); **Alamy Stock Photo:** Avalon / Photoshot License 104 (deforestation), Will Bailey 108 (pop), Greg Balfour Evans 26/2, 106 (newsagent), Guy Bell 108 (rock), Christian Bertrand 108 (reggae), Stuart Black 106 (supermarket), British Retail Photography 26/3, 106 (chemist), Ian Canham 106 (university), Tom Croke 109 (gardens), Cultura Creative (RF) 109 (aquarium), Adrian Davies 22tl, DBURKE 106 (urban), Vlad Deep 110 (mirror), Peter Etchells 109 (water park), Everett Collection Inc 108 (blues), Alexander Farmer 109 (museum), geogphotos 26/1, 106 (factory), imageBROKER 111 (wax), incamerastock 106 (post office), Justin Kase zsixz 28 (a), 106 (police station), Haje Jan Kamps 26/4, 106 (college), Paul King 107 (curry), Russell Kord 28 (f), 106 (guest house), Alexey Kostin 110 (rocket), LH Images 109 (pirate ship), Lin-Ann Lim 28 (c), 106 (underground), Maki Studio 111 (donate food), Tom McGahan 53tr, Mark Mercer 106 (bus stop), Mode Images 104 (first aid kit), PhotoCuisine RM 107 (omelette), PHOTOINKE 111 (car pool), Prisma by Dukas Presseagentur GmbH 104 (tribes), Purestock 110 (space station), Alex Segre 28 (d), 106 (bookshop), 107 (fish and chips), The Photolibrary Wales 28 (e), 106 (fire station), 106 (stadium), Sergiy Tryapitsyn 111 (keep the planet clean), Colin Underhill 28 (b), 106 (airport), Valentyn Volkov 107 (balanced), ZUMA Press Inc 108 (country); Fotolia.com: arbaes 26/7, 106 (theatre), Peter Baxter 106 (circus), creativenature.nl 69/1, Liping Dong 22tr, 105 (dinosaur), Eric Isselée 105 (camel), Veniamin Kraskov 104 (tent), Monkey Business 107 (lifestyle), Hazel Proudlove 107 (portions), Sabphoto 34l, Silkstock 91, Skogas 107 (physical exercise), stocker1970 106 (rural), Richard Villalon 104 (pump); **Getty Images:** Corbis / VCG / Monalyn Gracia 110 (reflection), DaddyBit 105 (rhino), GlobalP 105 (cheetah), GMVozd 107 (spaghetti), Hill Street Studios 34r, imv 22tc, jrroman 22bl, monkeybusinessimages 107 (paella), Ariel Skelley 109 (boating lake); **Jupiterimages:** 25tr; **Pearson Education Ltd:** Jon Barlow 36, MindStudio 9, Miguel Domínguez Muñoz 15cl, Tudor Photography 28b, 104 (pegs); **Shutterstock.com:** Adisa 107 (sushi), 111 (reduce pollution), Africa Studio 109 (big wheel), Alex James Bramwell 105 (turtle), angelshot 111 (colony), Artens 106 (traffic), ArtTDi 104 (humid), AuntSpray 105 (dodo), Evgeniy Ayupov 105 (smallest), Mikhail Bakunovich 108 (drums), Paul Banton 19cl, 25br, biletskiy 111 (crop), bluebay 62/2, 109 (satellite), bouybin 104 (drought), Butterfly Hunter 105 (lightest), ChameleonsEye 53cr, Computer Earth 105 (biggest), 105 (whale), dezignor 110 (comet), DnDavis 15r, dotshock 109 (water slide), Chris Driscoll 19l, Christopher Elwell 105 (seal), Marisa Estivill 109 (national park), f9photos 104 (rucksack), fivespots 105 (longest), Robert Ford 109 (carousel), Gemenacom 111 (save resources), Gl0ck 110 (planet), GraphicsRF 104 (torch), Ruslan Grumble 108 (trumpet), Mark Herreid 104 (sleeping bag), Robert Adrian Hillman 62/3, 109 (pressure), irin-k 111 (species), Eric Isselee 105 (fastest), 105 (koala), 105 (otter), John Kasawa 104 (mattress), Cathy Keifer 22bc, Anne Kitzman 109 (mini golf), Kletr 105 (tallest), 111 (save trees), Jan Kratochvila 25tl, Ivan Kuzmin 19c, lalito 108 (clarinet), Jill Lang 109 (skyscraper), Robyn Mackenzie 108 (cello), mangostock 104 (conserving), Monkey Business Images 63b, 107 (rice and beans), Juanan Barros Moreno 111 (reduce waste), Brett Mulcahy 107 (stew), Gunter Nezhoda 106 (dirty), NothingIsEverything 108 (harmonica), nrey 105 (lemur), Four Oaks 25bl, OSORIOartist 62/5, 109 (thermometer), Claudia Otte 111 (conserve energy), Pablo77 109 (theme park), paleontologist natural 105 (palaeontologists), pandapaw 105 (tiger), Pavel K 62/6, 109 (humidity), Pertusinas 111 (survive), Richard Peterson 105 (heaviest), photobar 19r, pixfly 62/1, 109 (anemometer), Targn Pleiades 109 (castle), pryzmat 26/5, 106 (shopping centre), RemarkEliza 53l, rm 19cr, sanneberg 58, Elena Schweitzer 108 (triangle), Rohit Seth 15cr, Andrea Skjold Mink 107 (dumplings), Dmitry Skutin 108 (harp), Jo Ann Snover 106 (village), Eduard Stelmakh 107 (energy), Steve Photography 109 (dodgems), Becky Swora 111 (pollinate), Artur Synenko 62/4, 109 (barometer), szefei 104 (dense), Theastock 63t, Tsekhmister 105 (shortest), Ungor 106 (railway station), Vereshchagin Dmitry 108 (tambourine), Tracy Whiteside 64, xpixel 105 (slowest), Jerry Zitterman 109 (rollercoaster), Peter Zurek 26/6, 106 (cinema), Zyphrus 105 (structure)

All other images © Pearson Education

Every effort has been made to trace the copyright holders and we apologise in advance for any unintentional omissions. We would be pleased to insert the appropriate acknowledgement in any subsequent edition of this publication.